POETRY FOR CHILDREN

Look into our childish faces;
See you not our willing hearts?

The Children's Appeal.

Poetry for Children

EDITED BY

SAMUEL ELIOT

Granger Index Reprint Series

BOOKS FOR LIBRARIES PRESS
FREEPORT, NEW YORK

First Published 1879
Reprinted 1971

INTERNATIONAL STANDARD BOOK NUMBER:
0-8369-6268-0

LIBRARY OF CONGRESS CATALOG CARD NUMBER:
76-160905

PRINTED IN THE UNITED STATES OF AMERICA

PREFACE.

THE illustrations of this volume are by different hands. Some of them appear so helpful in interesting the reader as to call for cordial acknowledgment from the editor.

Many poems naturally looked for in a collection like this are omitted, because found in our School Readers.

The arrangement of these selections is intended to be elastic, changing from easier to harder pieces, and back again. It is also meant to be suggestive of the likeness or the difference between one poem and another, so as to quicken thought and feeling. Let us hope that every child in our Primary and Grammar classes will find something here to please him, and that the teachers will encourage the children, first, to read only what is suited to them, and, next, to commit what they read to memory, as the best means of exercising that faculty and kindling the whole intelligence.

May the love of poetry, and of the good that poetry teaches, be the portion of our children!

CONTENTS.

CONTENTS.

LIST OF ILLUSTRATIONS

THE CHILDREN'S APPEAL.

Give us light amid our darkness;
  Let us know the good from ill;
Hate us not for all our blindness;
Love us, lead us, show us kindness, —
  You can make us what you will.

We are willing; we are ready;
  We would learn if you would teach;
We have hearts that yearn towards duty;
We have minds alive to beauty;
  Souls that any heights can reach.

We shall be what you will make us: —
  Make us wise, and make us good;
Make us strong for time of trial;
Teach us temperance, self-denial,
  Patience, kindness, fortitude.

Look into our childish faces;
  See you not our willing hearts?
Only love us — only lead us;
Only let us know you need us,
  And we all will do our parts.

Train us; try us; days slide onward,
  They can ne'er be ours again:
Save us; save from our undoing;
Save from ignorance and ruin;
  Free us all from wrong and stain.

Send us to our loving mothers,
  Angel-stamped in heart and brow.
We may be our fathers' teachers;
We may be the mightiest preachers,
  In the day that dawneth now.

Such the children's mute appealing.
  All my inmost soul was stirred,
And my heart was bowed with sadness,
When a cry, like summer's gladness,
  Said, " The children's prayer is heard ! "

                                    MARY HOWITT.

INFANT JOY.

———

"I have no name,
I am but two days old."
What shall I call thee?
"I happy am,
Joy is my name."
Sweet joy befall thee!

Pretty Joy!
Sweet Joy, but two days old,
Sweet Joy I call thee:
Thou dost smile,
I sing the while;
Sweet joy befall thee!

BLAKE.

———o○:◦:○o———

ONLY A BABY SMALL.

———

Only a baby small,
   Dropt from the skies;
Only a laughing face,
   Two sunny eyes;

Only two cherry lips,
　One chubby nose;
Only two little hands,
　Ten little toes.

Only a golden head,
　Curly and soft;
Only a tongue that wags
　Loudly and oft;
Only a little brain,
　Empty of thought;
Only a little heart,
　Troubled with nought.

Only a tender flower,
  Sent us to rear ;
Only a life to love
  While we are here ;
Only a baby small,
  Never at rest ;
Small, but how dear to us,
  God knoweth best.

M. BARR.

———∘∘⦂⊛⦂∘∘———

PRETTY COW.

———

Thank you, pretty cow, that made
  Pleasant milk to soak my bread,
Every day and every night,
  Warm, and fresh, and sweet, and white.

Do not chew the hemlock rank,
  Growing on the weedy bank ;
But the yellow cowslips eat,
  That will make it very sweet.

Where the purple violet grows,
  Where the bubbling water flows,
Where the grass is fresh and fine,
  Pretty cow, go there and dine.

TWINKLE, TWINKLE, LITTLE STAR.

Twinkle, twinkle, little star ;
How I wonder what you are !
Up above the world so high,
Like a diamond in the sky.

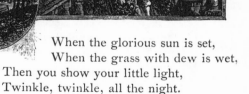

When the glorious sun is set,
When the grass with dew is wet,
Then you show your little light,
Twinkle, twinkle, all the night.

In the dark blue sky you keep,
And often through my curtains peep ;
For you never shut your eye
Till the sun is in the sky.

As your bright and tiny spark
Lights the traveller in the dark,
Though I know not what you are,
Twinkle, twinkle, little star.

————∘○⦂◉⦂○∘————

THE ROBIN REDBREASTS.

———

Two Robin Redbreasts built their nests
　Within a hollow tree ;
The hen sat quietly at home,
　The cock sang merrily ;
And all the little young ones said,
　"Wee, wee, wee, wee, wee, wee !"

One day (the sun was warm and bright,
　And shining in the sky)
Cock Robin said, " My little dears,
　'Tis time you learn to fly ;"
And all the little young ones said,
　" I'll try, I'll try, I'll try !"

I know a child, and who she is
　I'll tell you by-and-by,
When mamma says, " Do this," or " that,"
　She says, " What for ? " and " Why ? "
She'd be a better child by far
　If she would say, " I'll try."

AUNT EFFIE'S RHYMES.

THE CHILD'S HYMN.

We are poor and lowly born ;
  With the poor we bide ;
Labor is our heritage,
  Care and want beside.
What of this? — our blesséd Lord
  Was of lowly birth,
And poor toiling fishermen
  Were His friends on earth !

We are ignorant and young,
  Simple children all ;
Gifted with but humble powers,
  And of learning small.
What of this? — our blesséd Lord
  Lovéd such as we ;
How He blessed the little ones
  Sitting on His knee !

MARY HOWITT.

THE FAIRIES OF THE CALDON-LOW.

A MIDSUMMER LEGEND.

" And where have you been, my Mary,
    And where have you been from me? " —
" I've been to the top of the Caldon-Low,
    The midsummer night to see ! "

" And what did you see, my Mary,
    All up on the Caldon-Low? " —
" I saw the blithe sunshine come down,
    And I saw the merry winds blow."

" And what did you hear, my Mary,
    All up on the Caldon Hill? " —
" I heard the drops of the water made,
    And I heard the corn-ears fill."

" Oh, tell me all, my Mary —
    All, all that ever you know ;
  For you must have seen the fairies
    Last night on the Caldon-Low."

" Then take me on your knee, mother,
    And listen, mother of mine :
  A hundred fairies danced last night,
    And the harpers they were nine ;

"And merry was the glee of the harp-strings,
    And their dancing feet so small ;
  But, oh ! the sound of their talking
    Was merrier far than all ! "

"And what were the words, my Mary,
    That you did hear them say ? " —
" I'll tell you all, my mother,
    But let me have my way.

"And some they played with the water,
    And rolled it down the hill ;
  'And this,' they said, ' shall speedily turn
    The poor old miller's mill ;

" ' For there has been no water
    Ever since the first of May ;
  And a busy man shall the miller be
    By the dawning of the day !

" ' Oh, the miller, how he will laugh,
    When he sees the mill-dam rise !
  The jolly old miller, how he will laugh
    Till the tears fill both his eyes ! '

"And some they seized the little winds,
    That sounded over the hill,
And each put a horn into his mouth,
    And blew so sharp and shrill : —

" 'And there,' said they, ' the merry winds go
    Away from every horn ;
And those shall clear the mildew dank
    From the blind old widow's corn :

" ' Oh, the poor blind widow —
    Though she has been blind so long,
She'll be merry enough when the mildew's gone,
    And the corn stands stiff and strong ! '

"And some they brought the brown linseed,
    And flung it down from the Low :
'And this,' said they, ' by the sunrise,
    In the weaver's croft shall grow !

" ' Oh, the poor lame weaver !
    How he will laugh outright
When he sees his dwindling flax-field
    All full of flowers by night ! '

"And then upspoke a brownie,
    With a long beard on his chin :
' I have spun up all the tow,' said he,
    'And I want some more to spin.

" ' I've spun a piece of hempen cloth,
    And I want to spin another —
A little sheet for Mary's bed,
    And an apron for her mother ! '

" And with that I could not help but laugh,
    And I laughed out loud and free ;
And then on top of the Caldon-Low
    There was no one left but me.

" And all on top of the Caldon-Low
    The mists were cold and gray,
  And nothing I saw but the mossy stones
    That round about me lay.

" But, as I came down from the hill-top,
    I heard, afar below,
  How busy the jolly miller was,
    And how merry the wheel did go.

" And I peeped into the widow's field,
    And sure enough were seen
  The yellow ears of the mildewed corn
    All standing stiff and green !

" And down by the weaver's croft I stole,
    To see if the flax were high ;
  But I saw the weaver at his gate,
    With the good news in his eye !

" Now this is all I heard, mother,
    And all that I did see ;
  So, prithee, make my bed, mother,
    For I'm tired as I can be ! "

                              MARY HOWITT.

THE LITTLE DOVES.

High on the top of an old pine-tree
Broods a mother-dove with her young ones three.
Warm over them is her soft, downy breast,
And they sing so sweetly in their nest.
" Coo," say the little ones, " Coo," says she,
All in their nest on the old pine-tree.

Soundly they sleep through the moonshiny night,
Each young one covered and tucked in tight;
Morn wakes them up with the first blush of light,
And they sing to each other with all their might.
" Coo," say the little ones, etc.

When in the nest they are all left alone,
While their mother far for their dinner has flown,
Quiet and gentle they all remain,
Till their mother they see come home again.
Then " Coo," etc.

When they are fed by their tender mother,
One never will push nor crowd another:
Each opens widely his own little bill,
And he patiently waits, and gets his fill.
Then " Coo," etc.

Wisely the mother begins by and by
To make her young ones learn to fly ;
Just for a little way over the brink,
Then back to the nest as quick as a wink.
And " Coo," etc.

Fast grow the young ones, day and night,
Till their wings are plumed for a longer flight ;
Till unto the mat the last draws nigh
The time when they all must say " Good-by."
Then " Coo," say the little ones, " Coo," says she,
And away they fly from the old pine-tree.

CAROLS, HYMNS, AND SONGS.

THE CHIMNEY-SWEEP.

" Sweep ho !   Sweep ho !"
He trudges on through sleet and snow.

Tired and hungry both is he,
And he whistles vacantly.

Sooty black his rags and skin,
But the child is fair within.

Ice and cold are better far
Than his master's curses are.

Mother of this little one,
Couldst thou see thy little son!

"Sweep ho! Sweep ho!"
He trudges on through sleet and snow.

At the great man's door he knocks,
Which the servant-maid unlocks.

Now let in with laugh and jeer,
In his eye there stands a tear.

He is young, but soon will know
How to bear both word and blow.

" Sweep ho ! Sweep ho ! "
In the chimney, sleet, and snow.

Gladly, should his task be done,
Were't the last beneath the sun.

Faithfully it now shall be :
But, soon spent, down droppeth he ;

Gazes round, as in a dream ;
Very strange, but true, things seem.

Creeps he to a little bed,
Pillows there his aching head ;

And, poor thing ! he does not know
There he lay long years ago.

MRS. HOOPER.

THE

DEATH OF MASTER TOMMY ROOK.

A pair of steady rooks
Chose the safest of all nooks,
In the hollow of a tree to build their home ;
And while they kept within
They did not care a pin
For any roving sportsman that might come.

Their family of five
Were all happy and alive ;
And Mrs. Rook was careful as could be
To never let them out,
Till she looked all round about,
And saw that they might wander far and free.

She had talked to every one
Of the dangers of a gun,
And fondly begged that none of them would stir
To take a distant flight,
At morning, noon, or night,
Before they prudently asked leave of her.

But one fine sunny day,
Towards the end of May,
Young Tommy Rook began to scorn
her power,
And said that he would fly
Into the field close by,
And walk among the daisies for an hour.

"Stop, stop!" she cried, alarmed.
"I see a man that's armed,
And he will shoot you, sure as you are seen;
Wait till he goes, and then,
Secure from guns and men,
We all will have a ramble on the green."

But Master Tommy Rook,
With a very saucy look,
Perched on a twig, and plumed his jetty breast;
Still talking all the while,
In a very pompous style,
Of doing just what he might like the best.

" I don't care one bit," said he,
  " For any gun you see ;
I am tired of the cautions you bestow :
    I mean to have my way,
    Whatever you may say,
And shall not ask when I may stay or go."

  " But, my son," the mother cried,
    " I only wish to guide
Till you are wise and fit to go alone :
    I have seen much more of life,
    Of danger, woe, and strife,
Than you, my child, can possibly have known.

  "Just wait ten minutes here, —
    Let that man disappear ;
I am sure he means to do some evil thing ;
    I fear you may be shot
    If you leave this sheltered spot ;
So pray come back, and keep beside my wing."

  But Master Tommy Rook
    Gave another saucy look,
And chattered out, "Don't care ! don't care ! don't care !"
    And off he flew with glee,
    From his brothers in the tree,
And lighted on the field so green and fair.

He hopped about, and found
All pleasant things around ;
He strutted through the daisies, — but, alas !
A loud shot — bang ! — was heard,
And the wounded, silly bird
Rolled over, faint and dying, on the grass.

" There, there, I told you so ! "
Cried his mother in her woe,
" I warned you with a parent's thoughtful truth ;
And you see that I was right
When I tried to stop your flight,
And said you needed me to guide your youth."

Poor Master Tommy Rook
Gave a melancholy look,
And cried, just as he drew his latest breath :
" Forgive me, mother dear,
And let my brothers hear
That disobedience caused my cruel death."

Now, when his lot was told,
The rooks, both young and old,
All said he should have done as he was bid, —
That he well deserved his fate ;
And I, who now relate
His hapless story, really think he did.

ELIZA COOK.

MY GOOD-FOR-NOTHING.

———

" What are you good for, my brave little man?
Answer that question for me, if you can, —
You, with your fingers as white as a nun, —
You, with your ringlets as bright as the sun.
All the day long, with your busy contriving,
Into all mischief and fun you are driving :
See if your wise little noddle can tell
What you are good for.   Now, ponder it well."

Over the carpet the dear little feet
Came with a patter to climb on my seat ;
Two merry eyes, full of frolic and glee,
Under their lashes looked up unto me ;
Two little hands, pressing soft on my face,
Drew me down close in a loving embrace ;
Two rosy lips gave the answer so true,
" Good to love you, mamma, — good to love you."

POSIES FOR CHILDREN.

CHILDREN IN THE MOON

Hearken, child, unto a story!
    For the moon is in the sky,
And across her shield of silver
    See two tiny cloudlets fly.

Watch them closely, mark them sharply,
    As across the light they pass:
Seem they not to have the figures
    Of a little lad and lass?

See, my child, across their shoulders
 Lies a little pole! and lo!
Yonder speck is just the bucket
 Swinging softly to and fro.

It is said these little children,
 Many and many a summer night,
To a little well far northward
 Wandered in the still moonlight.

To the wayside-well they trotted,
 Filled their little buckets there;
And the moon-man, looking downward,
 Saw how beautiful they were.

Quoth the man, " How vexed and sulky
 Looks the little rosy boy!
But the little handsome maiden
 Trips behind him full of joy.

"To the well behind the hedgerow
 Trot the little lad and maiden;
From the well behind the hedgerow
 Now the little pail is laden.

" How they please me ! how they tempt me !
  Shall I snatch them up to-night? —
Snatch them, set them here forever
  In the middle of my light?

" Children, ay, and children's children,
  Should behold my babes on high ;
And my babes should smile forever,
  Calling others to the sky ! "

Never is the bucket empty,
  Never are the children old, —
Ever when the moon is shining
  We the children may behold.

KITTY IN THE BASKET.

"Where is my little basket gone?"
 Said Charlie boy one day.
"I guess some little boy or girl
 Has taken it away.

"And kitty, too, I can't find her.
 Oh, dear, what shall I do?
I wish I could my basket find,
 And little kitty too.

"I'll go to mother's room and look;
 Perhaps she may be there,
For kitty loves to take a nap
 In mother's easy-chair.

"O mother! mother! come and look!
 See what a little heap!
My kitty's in the basket here,
 All cuddled down to sleep."

He took the basket carefully,
 And brought it in a minute,
And showed it to his mother dear,
 With little kitty in it.

MRS. FOLLEN.

PUSSY-CAT.

Pussy-cat lives in the servants' hall,
  She can set up her back and purr;
The little mice live in a crack in the wall,
  But they hardly dare venture to stir;

For whenever they think of taking the air,
  Or filling their little maws,
The pussy-cat says, " Come out if you dare;
  I will catch you all with my claws."

Scrabble, scrabble, scrabble! went all the little mice,
  For they smelt the Cheshire cheese;
The pussy-cat said, " It smells very nice;
  Now do come out, if you please."

" Squeak!" said the little mouse. " Squeak, squeak,
    squeak!"
  Said all the young ones too, —
" We never creep out when cats are about,
  Because we're afraid of you."

So the cunning old cat lay down on a mat
  By the fire in the servants' hall:
" If the little mice peep they'll think I'm asleep;"
  So she rolled herself up like a ball.

" Squeak ! " said the little mouse ; " **we'll creep out**
    And eat some Cheshire cheese :
That silly old cat is asleep on the mat,
    And we may sup at our ease."

Nibble, nibble, nibble ! went all the little mice,
    And they licked their little paws ;
Then the cunning old cat sprang up from the mat,
    And caught them all with her claws.

AUNT EFFIE'S RHYMES.

LITTLE   WHITE   LILY.

———

Little white Lily
  Sat by a stone,
Drooping and waiting
  Till the sun shone.
Little white Lily
  Sunshine has fed ;
Little white Lily
  Is lifting her head.

Little white Lily
  Said, " It is good ;
Little white Lily's
  Clothing and food."
Little white Lily
  Drest like a bride !
Shining with whiteness,
  And crowned beside !

Little white Lily
  Droopeth with pain,
Waiting and waiting
  For the wet rain.

Little white Lily
　　Holdeth her cup ;
Rain is fast falling
　　And filling it up.

Little white Lily
　　Said, " Good again,
When I am thirsty
　　To have fresh rain.
Now I am stronger,
　　Now I am cool ;
Heat cannot burn me,
　　My veins are so full."

Little white Lily
　　Smells very sweet ;
On her head sunshine,
　　Rain at her feet.
Thanks to the sunshine,
　　Thanks to the rain !
Little white Lily
　　Is happy again !

GEORGE MACDONALD.

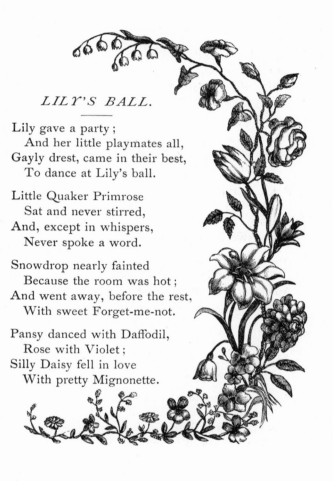

LILY'S BALL.

Lily gave a party ;
  And her little playmates all,
Gayly drest, came in their best,
  To dance at Lily's ball.

Little Quaker Primrose
  Sat and never stirred,
And, except in whispers,
  Never spoke a word.

Snowdrop nearly fainted
  Because the room was hot ;
And went away, before the rest,
  With sweet Forget-me-not.

Pansy danced with Daffodil,
  Rose with Violet ;
Silly Daisy fell in love
  With pretty Mignonette.

But, when they danced the country-dance,
  One could scarcely tell
Which of these two danced it best, —
  Cowslip or Heatherbell.

Between the dances, when they all
  Were seated in their places,
I thought I'd never seen before
  So many pretty faces.

But, of all the pretty maidens
  I saw at Lily's ball,
Darling Lily was to me
  The sweetest of them all.

And, when the dance was over,
  They went downstairs to sup ;
And each had a taste of honey-cake,
  With dew in a buttercup.

And all were dressed to go away,
  Before the set of sun ;
And Lily said " Good-by," and gave
  A kiss to every one.

And before the moon or a single star
  Was shining overhead,
Lily and all her little friends
  Were fast asleep in bed.

FUN AND EARNEST.

THE POPPY.

High on a bright and sunny bed
  A scarlet poppy grew ;
And up it held its staring head,
  And thrust it full in view.

Yet no attention did it win
  By all these efforts made,
And less unwelcome had it been
  In some retired shade.

For though within its scarlet breast
  No sweet perfume was found,
It seemed to think itself the best
  Of all the flowers around.

From this I may a hint obtain,
  And take great care indeed,
Lest I appear as pert and vain
  As is this gaudy weed.

                    JANE TAYLOR.

LITTLE DANDELION.

Gay little Dandelion
  Lights up the meads,
Swings on her slender foot,
  Telleth her beads,
Lists to the robin's note
  Poured from above ;
Wise little Dandelion
  Asks not for love.

Cold lie the daisy banks
  Clothed but in green,
Where, in the days agone,
  Bright hues were seen.
Wild pinks are slumbering,
  Violets delay ;
True little Dandelion
  Greeteth the May.

Brave little Dandelion !
  Fast falls the snow,
Bending the daffodil's
  Haughty head low.

Under that fleecy tent,
  Careless of cold,
Blithe little Dandelion
  Counteth her gold.

Meek little Dandelion
  Groweth more fair,
Till dies the amber dew
  Out from her hair.
High rides the thirsty sun,
  Fiercely and high ;
Faint little Dandelion
  Closeth her eye.

Pale little Dandelion,
  In her white shroud,
Heareth the angel-breeze
  Call from the cloud !
Tiny plumes fluttering
  Make no delay ;
Little winged Dandelion
  Soareth away.

Helen B. Bostwick.

THE VIOLET.

Down in a green and shady bed
  A modest violet grew ;
Its stalk was bent, it hung its head,
  As if to hide from view.

And yet it was a lovely flower,
  Its colors bright and fair !
It might have graced a rosy bower,
  Instead of hiding there.

Yet there it was content to bloom,
  In modest tints arrayed ;
And there diffused its sweet perfume
  Within the silent shade.

Then let me to the valley go,
  This pretty flower to see,
That I may also learn to grow
  In sweet humility.

JANE TAYLOR.

THE RACE OF THE FLOWERS.

The trees and the flowers seem running a race,
  But none treads down the other ;
And neither thinks it his disgrace
  To be later than his brother.
Yet the pear-tree shouts to the lilac-tree,
  " Make haste, for the spring is late ! "
And the lilac-tree whispers to the chestnut-tree
  (Because he is so great),
" Pray you, great sir, be quick, be quick,
For down below we are blossoming thick ! "

Then the chestnut hears, and comes out in bloom,
  White or pink, to the tip-top boughs :
Oh ! why not grow higher, there's plenty of room,
  You beautiful tree, with the sky for your house ?
Then, like music, they seem to burst out together,
  The little and the big, with a beautiful burst ;
They sweeten the wind, they paint the weather,
  And no one remembers which was first, —
      White rose, red rose,
      Bud rose, shed rose,

    Larkspur and lily, and the rest;
    North, east, south, west,
    June, July, August, September!
Ever so late in the year will come
Many a red geranium,
    And chrysanthemums up to November!
Then the winter has overtaken them all,
The fogs and the rains begin to fall;
And the flowers, after running their races,
Are weary and shut up their faces,
And under the ground they go to sleep.
" Is it very far down?" — " Yes, ever so deep."

LILLIPUT LEVEE.

—o∘⟐∘o—

A LITTLE GOOSE.

The chill November day was done,
    The working world home faring;
The wind came roaring through the streets,
    And set the gaslights flaring;
And hopelessly and aimlessly
    The scared old leaves were flying, —
When, mingled with the soughing wind,
    I heard a small voice crying.

And, shivering on the corner, stood
　A child of four, or over ;
No cloak or hat her small soft arms
　And wind-blown curls to cover ;

Her dimpled face was stained with tears ;
　Her round blue eyes ran over ;
She cherished in her wee, cold hand
　A bunch of faded clover.

And, one hand round her treasure, while
  She slipped in mine the other,
Half-scared, half-confidential, said,
  " Oh ! please, I want my mother." —
" Tell me your street and number, pet.
  Don't cry : I'll take you to it."
Sobbing, she answered, " I forget :
  The organ made me do it.

" He came and played at Miller's step, —
  The monkey took the money ;
I followed down the street because
  That monkey was so funny.
I've walked about a hundred hours
  From one street to another ;
The monkey's gone ; I've spoiled my flowers ; —
  Oh, please, I want my mother."

" But what's your mother's name ? and what
  The street ? Now think a minute." —
" My mother's name is Mother Dear ;
  The street — I can't begin it." —
" But what is strange about the house,
  Or new, — not like the others ? " —
" I guess you mean my trundle-bed, —
  Mine and my little brother's.

" Oh dear ! I ought to be at home
   To help him say his prayers, —
He's such a baby he forgets ;
   And we are both such players ;
And there's a bar between to keep
   From pitching on each other,
For Harry rolls when he's asleep ;
   Oh dear ! I want my mother."

The sky grew stormy ; people passed
   All muffled, homeward faring.
" You'll have to spend the night with me,"
   I said at last, despairing.
I tied a kerchief round her neck :
   " What ribbon's this, my blossom ? " —
" Why, don't you know ? " she, smiling, said,
   And drew it from her bosom.

A card with number, street, and name !
   My eyes, astonished, met it ;
"For," said the little one, " you see
   I might some time forget it,
And so I wear a little thing
   That tells you all about it ;
For mother says she's very sure
   I should get lost without it."

ELIZA S. TURNER.

MARY'S LAMB.

Mary had a little lamb,
　　Its fleece was white as snow ;
And everywhere that Mary went,
　　The lamb was sure to go.

He followed her to school one day, —
　　That was against the rule ;
It made the children laugh and play,
　　To see a lamb at school.

So the teacher turned him out,
　　But still he lingered near,
And waited patiently about,
　　Till Mary did appear.

Then he ran to her, and laid
　　His head upon her arm,
As if he said, " I'm not afraid, —
　　You'll keep me from all harm."

" What makes the lamb love Mary so ? "
　　The eager children cry.
" Oh, Mary loves the lamb, you know,"
　　The teacher did reply.

MRS. HALE.

THE PET LAMB.

The dew was falling fast, the stars began to blink;
I heard a voice: it said, " Drink, pretty creature.
    drink !"
And, looking o'er the hedge, before me I espied
A snow-white mountain lamb, with a maiden at its side.

No other sheep were near, the lamb was all alone,
And by a slender cord was tethered to a stone ;
With one knee on the grass did the little maiden kneel,
While to that mountain lamb she gave its evening meal.

The lamb, while from her hand he thus his supper took,
Seemed to feast with head and ears ; and his tail with
    pleasure shook.
" Drink, pretty creature, drink," she said in such a tone,
That I almost received her heart into my own.

'Twas little Barbara Lewthwaite, a child of beauty rare !
I watched them with delight: they were a lovely pair.
Now with her empty can the maiden turned away ;
But, ere ten yards were gone, her footsteps did she stay.

Towards the lamb she looked; and from that shady
    place
I, unobserved, could see the workings of her face:
If Nature to her tongue could measured numbers bring,
Thus, thought I, to her lamb that little maid might
    sing : —

" What ails thee, young one? What? Why pull so at
    thy cord?
Is it not well with thee? well both for bed and board?
Thy plot of grass is soft, and green as grass can be;
Rest, little young one, rest: what is't that aileth thee?

" Rest, little young one, rest; thou hast forgot the day
When my father found thee first in places far away:
Many flocks were on the hills, but thou wert owned by
    none,
And thy mother from thy side for evermore was gone.

" He took thee in his arms, and in pity brought thee
    home :
A blessed day for thee! Then whither wouldst thou
    roam?
A faithful nurse thou hast: the dam that did thee yean
Upon the mountain-tops no kinder could have been.

" Thou know'st that twice a day I have brought thee in
this can
Fresh water from the brook, as clear as ever ran ;
And twice in the day, when the ground is wet with dew,
I bring thee draughts of milk, — warm milk it is and
new.

" It will not, will not rest ! — poor creature, can it be
That 'tis thy mother's heart which is working so in
thee ?
Things that I know not of belike to thee are dear,
And dreams of things which thou canst neither see nor
hear."

As homeward through the lane I went with lazy feet,
This song to myself did I oftentimes repeat ;
And it seemed, as I retraced the ballad line by line,
That but half of it was hers, and one-half of it was mine.

Again, and once again, did I repeat the song ;
" Nay," said I, " more than half to the damsel must
belong,
For she looked with such a look, and she spake with such
a tone,
That I almost received her heart into mine own."

WORDSWORTH.

POOR SUSAN.

At the corner of Wood Street, when daylight appears,
There's a thrush that sings loud, — it has sung for three
     years ;
Poor Susan has passed by the spot, and has heard
In the silence of morning the song of the bird.

'Tis a note of enchantment ; what ails her ? She sees
A mountain ascending, a vision of trees ;
Bright volumes of vapor through Lothbury glide,
And a river flows on through the vale of Cheapside.

Green pastures she views in the midst of the dale,
Down which she so often has tripped with her pail ;
And a single small cottage, a nest like a dove's,
The one only dwelling on earth that she loves.

She looks, and her heart is in heaven ; but they fade, —
The mist and the river, the hill and the shade :
The stream will not flow, and the hill will not rise,
And the colors have all passed away from her eyes.

WORDSWORTH.

LUCY GRAY; OR, SOLITUDE.

Oft have I heard of Lucy Gray;
　And, when I crossed the wild,
I chanced to see, at break of day,
　The solitary child.

No mate, no comrade, Lucy knew;
　She dwelt on a wide moor,
The sweetest thing that ever grew
　Beside a human door.

" To-night will be a stormy night, —
   You to the town must go ;
And take a lantern, child, to light
   Your mother through the snow."

" That, father, will I gladly do :
   'Tis scarcely afternoon, —
The minster clock has just struck two,
   And yonder is the moon."

At this the father raised his hook
   And snapped a fagot band ;
He plied his work ; and Lucy took
   The lantern in her hand.

Not blither is the mountain roe ;
   With many a wanton stroke
Her feet disperse the powdery snow,
   That rises up like smoke.

The storm came on before its time :
   She wandered up and down,
And many a hill did Lucy climb,
   But never reached the town.

The wretched parents all that night
   Went shouting far and wide ;
But there was neither sound nor sight
   To serve them for a guide.

At daybreak on a hill they stood
   That overlooked the moor,
And thence they saw the bridge of wood,
   A furlong from their door.

You yet may spy the fawn at play,
   The hare upon the green;
But the sweet face of Lucy Gray
   Will never more be seen.

And, turning homeward, now they cried.
   " In heaven we all shall meet ! "
When in the snow the mother spied
   The print of Lucy's feet.

Then downward from the steep hill's edge
   They tracked the footmarks small,
And through the broken hawthorn hedge,
   And by the long stone wall;

And then an open field they crossed:
   The marks were still the same;
They tracked them on, nor ever lost;
   And to the bridge they came.

They followed from the snowy bank
   The footmarks one by one,
Into the middle of the plank;
   And farther were there none !

Yet some maintain that to this day
　　She is a living child, —
That you may see sweet Lucy Gray
　　Upon the lonesome wild.

O'er rough and smooth she trips along,
　　And never looks behind,
And sings a solitary song
　　That whistles in the wind.

WORDSWORTH.

THE DYING CHILD.

A little child lay on his bed
　　And drew a heavy breath,
And moaning raised his weary head,
　　Damp with the dews of death.
Upon his bed the sunset cast
　　The broad and yellow ray
That oft in pleasant evenings past
　　Had warned him from his play.
He clasped his mother's hand and sighed,
　　And to his lip arose
A little prayer he learnt beside
　　Her knee at even's close.

And thus he prayed, ere darkness stole
  Upon the silence deep,
The Blessed One to keep his soul
  And guard him in his sleep : —

"*Ah! gentle Jesus, meek and mild,*
Look down on me, a little child;
Ah! pity my simplicity,
And grant me grace to come to Thee!

"*Four corners are around my bed,*
At every one an angel spread;
One to lead me, one to feed me,
Two to take my soul to heaven.

"And they will take it soon ; I know
  I have not long to wait,
Ere with those Shining Ones I go
  Within the pearly gate ;

"Ere I shall look upon His face
  Who died that I might live
With Him forever, through the grace
  That none save He can give !

"I go where the happy waters flow
  By the city of our King,
Where never cometh pain nor woe,
  Nor any evil thing.

" I go to play beneath the tree
    Upon whose branches high
The pleasant fruits of healing be,
    That none may taste and die.

" I go to join the blesséd throng
    Who walk arrayed in white,
To learn of them the holy song
    That rises day and night.

" I see them by the emerald light
    Shed by the living Bow :
Young seraph faces, pure and bright,
    More fair than aught below !

" Oh ! come to me, ye blesséd ones,
    And take me in your arms :
I know you by your shining robes,
    And by your waving palms.

" Your smiles are sweet as is the babe's
    Upon my mother's knee ;
O little one ! I would that thou
    Wert there along with me !

" How happily our days would flow
    Where all is glad and fair !
Ah ! might the faces that I know
    But look upon me *there!*

" For something dear will fail awhile
   In those abodes of bliss, —
The sweetness of my mother's smile,
   My father's evening kiss.

" If they will miss me on the earth,
   I shall miss them above,
And 'mid the holy angel mirth
   Shall think on those I love.

" But when they come I shall be first
   To give them welcome sweet;
My voice shall swell the joyous burst
   That doth the ransomed greet!

" I come, O Saviour! yes, I haste
   Thy ransomed child to be,
Yet I have many on the earth,
   And none in heaven but Thee!"

And then a Voice spake soft and clear,
   " Whom wouldst thou have but Me?
Who, in the heavens or with thee here,
   Hath owned such love for thee?"

.   .   .   .

And the child folded his wan hands, and smiled
As o'er a blissful meaning; but his breath
Failed in the happy utterance, as he met
His Father's kiss upon the lip of Death.

DORA GREENWELL.

THE REAPER AND THE FLOWERS.

There is a reaper whose name is Death,
    And, with his sickle keen,
He reaps the bearded grain at a breath,
    And the flowers that grow between.

" Shall I have nought that is fair ? " saith he ;
    " Have nought but the bearded grain?
Though the breath of these flowers is sweet to me,
    I will give them all back again."

He gazed at the flowers with tearful eyes,
    He kissed their drooping leaves ;
It was for the Lord of Paradise
    He bound them in his sheaves.

" My Lord has need of these flowerets gay,"
    The reaper said, and smiled ;
" Dear tokens of the earth are they,
    Where he was once a child.

" They shall all bloom in fields of light,
    Transplanted by my care,
And saints, upon their garments white,
    These sacred blossoms wear."

And the mother gave, in tears and pain,
  The flowers she most did love;
She knew she should find them all again
  In the fields of light above.

Oh, not in cruelty, not in wrath,
  The reaper came that day;
'Twas an angel visited the green
      earth,
  And took the flowers away.

LONGFELLOW.

LULLABY ON AN INFANT CHIEF.

Oh, hush thee, my baby, thy sire was a knight,
Thy mother a lady, both lovely and bright;
The woods and the glens, from the towers we see,
They all are belonging, dear baby, to thee.

Oh, fear not the bugle, though loudly it blows,
It calls but the warders that guard thy repose;
Their bows would be bended, their blades would be red,
Ere the step of a foeman draws near to thy bed.

Oh, hush thee, my baby, the time will soon come
When thy sleep shall be broken by trumpet and drum;
Then hush thee, my darling, take rest while you may,
For strife comes with manhood, and waking with day.

SCOTT.

THE SPARTAN BOY.

When I the memory repeat
Of the heroic actions great,
Which, in contempt of pain and death,
Were done by men who drew their breath

In ages past, I find no deed
That can in fortitude exceed
The noble boy, in Sparta bred,
Who in the temple ministered.
By the sacrifice he stands,
The lighted incense in his hands ;
Through the smoking censer's lid
Dropped a burning coal, which slid
Into his sleeve, and passed in
Between the folds, e'en to the skin.
Dire was the pain which then he proved,
But not for this his sleeve he moved,
Or would the scorching ember shake
Out from the folds, lest it should make
Any confusion, or excite
Disturbance at the sacred rite ;
But close he kept the burning coal,
Till it eat itself a hole
In his flesh.   The standers-by
Saw no sign, and heard no cry,
All this he did in noble scorn,
And for he was a Spartan born.

MARY LAMB.

NELL AND HER BIRD.

GOOD-BY, little birdie!
    Fly to the sky,
Singing and singing
    A merry good-by.

Tell all the birdies
    Flying above,
Nell, in the garden,
    Sends them her love.

Tell how I found you,
    Hurt, in a tree;
Then, when they're wounded,
    They'll come right to me.

I'd like to go with you,
    If I could fly;
It must be so beautiful
    Up in the sky!

Why, little birdie —
    Why don't you go?
You sit on my finger,
    And shake your head, " No!"

He's off!   Oh, how quickly
   And gladly he rose !
I know he will love me
   Wherever he goes.

I know — for he really
   Seemed trying to say :
" My dear little Nelly,
   I can't go away."

But just then some birdies
   Came flying along,
And sang, as they neared us,
   A chirruping song ;

And he felt just as I do
   When girls come and shout
Right under the window,
   " Come, Nelly — come out ! "

It's wrong to be sorry ;
   I ought to be glad ;
But he's the best birdie
   That ever I had.

                              Mrs. Dodge.

THE SAILOR'S MOTHER.

One morning (raw it was and wet,
   A foggy day in winter-time)
A woman on the road I met,
   Not old, though something past her prime ;
Majestic in her person, tall and straight,
And like a Roman matron's was her mien and gait.

The ancient spirit is not dead ;
   Old times, thought I, are breathing there ;
Proud was I that my country bred
   Such strength, a dignity so fair.
She begged an alms, like one in poor estate.
I looked at her again, nor did my pride abate.

When from these lofty thoughts I woke,
   With the first word I had to spare
I said to her, "Beneath your cloak
   What's that which on your arms you bear?"
She answered, soon as she the question heard,
"A simple burden, sir, — a little singing-bird."

And thus continuing, she said,
    " I had a son, who many a day
Sailed on the seas : but he is dead ;
    In Denmark he was cast away ;
And I have travelled very far, to see
What clothes he might have left, or other property.

    " The bird and cage they both were his ;
       'Twas my son's bird ; and neat and trim
    He kept it : many voyages
       His singing-bird hath gone with him.
When last he sailed he left the bird behind ;
As it might be, perhaps, from bodings of his mind.

    " He to a fellow-lodger's care
       Had left it to be watched and fed,
    Till he came back again ; and there
       I found it when my son was dead ;
And now, — God help me for my little wit ! —
I trail it with me, sir ! he took so much delight in it."

WORDSWORTH.

LITTLE GIRL'S LAMENT.

Is Heaven a long way off, mother?
    I watch through all the day,
To see my father coming back
    And meet him on the way.

And when the night comes on I stand
    Where once I used to wait,
To see him coming from the fields
    And meet him at the gate;

Then I used to put my hand in his,
    And cared not more to play;
But I never meet him coming now,
    However long I stay.

And you tell me he's in Heaven, and far,
    Far happier than we,
And loves us still the same ; but how,
    Dear mother, can that be ?

For he never left a single day
    For market or for fair,
But the best of all that father saw
    He brought for us to share.

He cared for nothing then but us ;
    I have heard father say
That coming back made worth his while
    Sometimes to go away.

He used to say he liked our house
    Far better than the Hall ;
He would not change it for the best,
    The grandest place of all.

And if where he is now, mother,
    All is so good and fair,
He would have come back long ago
    To take us with him there.

He never would be missed from Heaven ;
    I have heard father say
How many angels God has there,
    To praise Him night and day ;

He never would be missed in Heaven,
  From all that blesséd throng.
And we — oh! we have missed him here
  So sadly and so long!

But if he came to fetch us, then
  I would hold his hand so fast,
I would not let it go again
  Till all the way was past.

He'd tell me all that he has seen,
  But I would never say
How dull and lonely we have been
  Since he went far away.

When you raised me to the bed, mother,
  And I kissed him on the cheek,
His cheek was pale and very cold,
  And his voice was low and weak.

And yet I can remember well
  Each word that he spoke then,
For he said I must be a dear, good girl,
  And we should meet again!

And, oh! but I have tried since then
  To be good through all the day;
I've done whate'er you bid me, mother,
  Yet father stays away!

Is it because God loves him so? —
  I know that in His love
He takes the good away from earth,
  To live with Him above!

Oh that God had not loved him so!
  For then he might have stayed,
And kissed me as he used at nights,
  When by his knee I played.

Oh that he had not been so good,
  So patient, or so kind!
Oh, had but we been more like him,
  And not been left behind!

DORA GREENWELL.

THE MAY QUEEN.

Part I.

You must wake and call me early, call me early, mother
    dear;
To-morrow'll be the happiest time of all the glad New
    Year;
Of all the glad New Year, mother, the maddest, merriest
    day;
For I'm to be Queen o' the May, mother, I'm to be
    Queen o' the May.

There's many a black, black eye, they say, but none so
    bright as mine ;
There's Margaret and Mary, there's Kate and Caroline ;
But none so fair as little Alice in all the land, they say ;
So I'm to be Queen o' the May, mother, I'm to be
    Queen o' the May.

I sleep so sound all night, mother, that I shall never
    wake,
If you do not call me loud, when the day begins to
    break :
But I must gather knots of flowers, and buds and gar-
    lands gay ;
For I'm to be Queen o' the May, mother, I'm to be
    Queen o' the May.

As I came up the valley, whom think you should I see,
But Robin, leaning on the bridge beneath the hazel tree?
He thought of that sharp look, mother, I gave him
    yesterday, —
But I'm to be Queen o' the May, mother, I'm to be
    Queen o' the May.

He thought I was a ghost, mother, for I was all in white,
And I ran by him without speaking, like a flash of light.

They call me cruel-hearted ; but I care not what they say,
For I'm to be Queen o' the May, mother, I'm to be
  Queen o' the May.

They say he's dying all for love ; but that can never be ;
They say his heart is breaking, mother ; what is that to
  me ?
There's many a bolder lad'll woo me any summer day,
For I'm to be Queen o' the May, mother, I'm to be
  Queen o' the May.

Little Effie shall go with me to-morrow to the green,
And you'll be there, too, mother, to see me made the
  queen ;
For the shepherd lads on every side'll come from far
  away,
And I'm to be Queen o' the May, mother, I'm to be
  Queen o' the May.

The honeysuckle round the porch has woven its wavy
  bowers,
And by the meadow-trenches blow the faint sweet
  cuckoo-flowers,
And the wild marsh-marigold shines like fire in swamps
  and hollows gray,
And I'm to be Queen o' the May, mother, I'm to be
  Queen o' the May.

The night-winds come and go, mother, upon the mead-
    ow-grass,
And the happy stars above them seem to brighten as they
    pass ;
There will not be a drop of rain the whole of the live-
    long day,
And I'm to be Queen o' the May, mother, I'm to be
    Queen o' the May.

All the valley, mother, 'll be fresh and green and still,
And the cowslip and the crowfoot are over all the hill,
And the rivulet in the flowery dale'll merrily glance
    and play ;
For I'm to be Queen o' the May, mother, I'm to be
    Queen o' the May.

So you must wake and call me early, call me early,
    mother dear ;
To-morrow'll be the happiest time of all the glad New
    Year ;
To-morrow'll be of all the year the maddest, merriest
    day ;
For I'm to be Queen o' the May, mother, I'm to be
    Queen o' the May.

Part II.

NEW YEAR'S EVE.

If you're waking, call me early, call me early, mother
dear,
For I would see the sun rise upon the glad New Year;
It is the last New Year that I shall ever see,
Then you may lay me low i' the mould, and think no
more of me.

To-night I saw the sun set: he set, and left behind
The good Old Year, the dear old time, and all my peace
of mind;
And the New Year's coming up, mother, but I shall
never see
The blossom on the blackthorn, the leaf upon the tree.

Last May we made a crown of flowers; we had a merry
day:
Beneath the hawthorn on the green they made me
Queen of May;
And we danced about the May-pole and in the hazel
copse,
Till Charles's Wain came out above the tall white
chimney-tops.

There's not a flower on all the hills : the frost is on
    the pane :
I only wish to live till the snow-drops come again :
I wish the snow would melt, and the sun come out on
    high :
I long to see a flower so before the day I die.

The building rook'll caw from the windy tall elm tree,
And the tufted plover pipe along the fallow lea,
And the swallow'll come back again with summer o'er
    the wave,
But I shall lie alone, mother, within the mouldering
    grave.

Upon the chancel casement, and upon that grave of
    mine,
In the early, early morning the summer sun'll shine,
Before the red cock crows from the farm upon the hill,
When you are warm asleep, mother, and all the world
    is still.

When the flowers come again, mother, beneath the
    waning light
You'll never see me more in the long gray fields at
    night ;

When from the dry dark wood the summer airs blow
    cool
On the oat-grass and the sword-grass, and the bulrush
    in the pool.

You'll bury me, my mother, just beneath the hawthorn
    shade,
And you'll come sometimes and see me where I am
    lowly laid.
I shall not forget you, mother ; I shall hear you when
    you pass,
With your feet above my head in the long and pleasant
    grass.

I have been wild and wayward, but you'll forgive me
    now ;
You'll kiss me, my own mother, upon my cheek and
    brow ; —
Nay, nay, you must not weep, nor let your grief be wild ;
You should not fret for me, mother, — you have another
    child.

If I can I'll come again, mother, from out my resting-
    place ;
Though you'll not see me, mother, I shall look upon
    your face ;

Though I cannot speak a word, I shall hearken what
you say,
And be often, often with you, when you think I'm far
away.

Good-night! good-night! When I have said good-night
for evermore,
And you see me carried out from the threshold of the
door,
Don't let Effie come to see me till my grave be growing green:
She'll be a better child to you than ever I have been.

She'll find my garden tools upon the granary floor:
Let her take 'em: they are hers: I shall never garden
more:
But tell her, when I'm gone, to train the rose-bush that I
set
About the parlor window, and the box of mignonette.

Good-night, sweet mother: call me before the day is
born.
All night I lie awake, but I fall asleep at morn;
But I would see the sun rise upon the glad New Year;
So, if you're waking, call me, call me early, mother
dear.

Part III.

CONCLUSION.

I thought to pass away before, and yet alive I am ;
And in the fields all round I hear the bleating of the
    lamb.
How sadly, I remember, rose the morning of the year !
To die before the snow-drop came, and now the violet's
    here.

Oh, sweet is the new violet that comes beneath the
    skies,
And sweeter is the young lamb's voice to me that cannot
    rise,
And sweet is all the land about, and all the flowers that
    blow,
And sweeter far is death than life to me that long to go !

It seemed so hard at first, mother, to leave the blesséd
    sun,
And now it seems as hard to stay ; and yet His will be
    done !
But still I think it can't be long before I find release ;
And that good man, the clergyman, has told me words
    of peace.

Oh, blessings on his kindly voice, and on his silver hair!
And blessings on his whole life long, until he meet me
there!
Oh, blessings on his kindly heart, and on his silver head!
A thousand times I blessed him, as he knelt beside my
bed.

He showed me all the mercy, for he taught me all the
sin:
Now, though my lamp was lighted late, there's One will
let me in:
Nor would I now be well, mother, again, if that could
be,
For my desire is but to pass to Him that died for me.

I did not hear the dog howl, mother, or the death-watch
beat,
There came a sweeter token when the night and morning
meet.
But sit beside my bed, mother, and put your hand in
mine,
And Effie on the other side, and I will tell the sign.

All in the wild March morning I heard the angels call:
It was when the moon was setting, and the dark was over
all;

The trees began to whisper, and the wind began to roll,
And in the wild March morning I heard them call my
soul.

For, lying broad awake, I thought of you and Effie dear;
I saw you sitting in the house, and I no longer here:
With all my strength I prayed for both, and so I felt
resigned,
And up the valley came a swell of music on the wind.

I thought that it was fancy, and I listened in my bed,
And then did something speak to me — I know not what
was said,
For great delight and shuddering took hold of all my
mind,
And up the valley came again the music on the wind.

But you were sleeping; and I said, "It's not for them:
it's mine."
And if it comes three times, I thought, I take it for a
sign.
And once again it came, and close beside the window-
bars,
Then seemed to go right up to Heaven, and die among
the stars.

So now I think my time is near. I trust it is. I know
The blessed music went that way my soul will have to
    go.
And for myself, indeed, I care not if I go to-day ;
But, Effie, you must comfort *her* when I am past away.

And say to Robin a kind word, and tell him not to fret :
There's many a worthier than I would make him happy
    yet.
If I had lived — I cannot tell — I might have been his
    wife ;
But all these things have ceased to be, with my desire
    of life.

Oh, look ! the sun begins to rise, the heavens are in a
    glow ;
He shines upon a hundred fields, and all of them I
    know.
And there I move no longer now, and there his light
    may shine —
Wild flowers in the valley for other hands than mine.

Oh, sweet and strange it seems to me, that ere this day
    is done
The voice, that now is speaking, may be beyond the
    sun —

Forever and forever with those just souls and true !
And what is life, that we should moan? why make we
     such ado?

Forever and forever, all in a blessed home,
And there to wait a little while till you and Effie come ;
To lie within the light of God, as I lie upon your
     breast,
And the wicked cease from troubling, and the weary
     are at rest.

TENNYSON.

———o·o:̣o·o———

ON ANOTHER'S SORROW.

Can I see another's woe,
And not be in sorrow too?
Can I see another's grief,
And not seek for kind relief ?

Can I see a falling tear,
And not feel my sorrow's share?
Can a father see his child
Weep, nor be with sorrow filled?

Can a mother sit and hear
An infant groan, an infant fear?
No ! no ! never can it be !
Never, never can it be !

And can He who smiles on all,
Hear the wren with sorrows small,
Hear the small bird's grief and care,
Hear the woes that infants bear, —

And not sit beside the nest,
Pouring pity in their breast?
And not sit the cradle near,
Weeping tear on infant's tear?

And not sit both night and day,
Wiping all our tears away?
Oh, no! never can it be!
Never, never can it be!

He doth give His joy to all;
He becomes an Infant small;
He becomes a Man of woe;
He doth feel the sorrow too.

Think not thou canst sigh a sigh,
And thy Maker is not nigh;
Think not thou canst weep a tear,
And thy Maker is not near.

Oh! He gives to us His joy,
That our griefs He may destroy;
Till our grief is fled and gone,
He doth sit by us and mourn.

BLAKE.

THE GLEANER.

Before the bright sun rises over the hill,
　　In the wheat-field poor Mary is seen,
Impatient her little blue apron to fill
　　With the few scattered ears she can glean.

She never leaves off or runs out of her place
　　To play or to idle and chat,
Except, now and then, just to wipe her hot face,
　　And fan herself with her broad hat.

" Poor girl ! hard at work in the heat of the sun,
　　How tired and warm you must be !
Why don't you leave off as the others have done,
　　And sit with them under the tree ? "

" Oh, no ! for my mother lies ill in her bed,
　　Too feeble to spin or to knit ;
And my dear little brothers are crying for bread,
　　And yet we can't give them a bit.

" Then could I be merry, be idle, or play,
　　While they are so hungry and ill?
Oh, no ! I would rather work hard all the day,
　　My little blue apron to fill."

JANE TAYLOR.

THE CHILDREN IN THE WOOD.

————

Now ponder well, you parents dear,
　　These words which I shall write ;
A doleful story you shall hear,
　　In time brought forth to light.

A gentleman of good account
　　In Norfolk dwelt of late,
Whose wealth and riches did **surmount**
　　Most men of his estate.

Sore sick he was, and like to die,
　　No help his life could save ;
His wife by him as sick did lie,
　　And both possess one grave.

No love between these two was lost, —
　　Each was to other kind ;
In love they lived, in love they died,
　　And left two babes behind :

The one a fine and pretty boy,
　　Not passing three years old ;
The other a girl more young than **he,**
　　And made in beauty's mould.

The father left his little son,
  As plainly doth appear,
When he to perfect age should come,
  Three hundred pounds a year.

And to his little daughter Jane
  Two hundred pounds in gold,
To be paid down on marriage-day,
  Which might not be controlled.

But if the children chanced to die
  Ere they to age should come,
Their uncle should possess their wealth, —
  For so the will did run.

" Now, brother," said the dying man,
  " Look to my children dear ;
Be good unto my boy and girl,
  No friends else have they here.

" To God and you I do commend
  My children night and day :
A little while be sure we have
  Within this world to stay.

" You must be father and mother both,
  And uncle, all in one ;
God knows what will become of them,
  When I am dead and gone."

With that bespake their mother dear,
  "O brother kind," quoth she,
"You are the man must bring my babes
  To wealth or misery:

  "If you do keep them carefully,
    Then God will you reward;
  If otherwise you seem to deal,
    God will your deeds regard."

With lips as cold as any stone
    They kissed the children small:
" God bless you both, my children dear ! " —
    With that the tears did fall.

These speeches then their brother spoke
    To this sick couple there :
" The keeping of your children dear,
    Sweet sister, do not fear.

" God never prosper me or mine,
    Nor aught else that I have,
If I do wrong your children dear,
    When you are laid in grave."

Their parents being dead and gone,
    The children home he takes,
And brings them both unto his house,
    And much of them he makes.

He had not kept those pretty babes
    A twelvemonth and a day,
When, for their wealth, he did devise
    To make them both away.

He bargained with two ruffians rude,
    Who were of furious mood,
That they should take the children young
    And slay them in the wood.

He told his wife, and all he knew,
　He would the children send
To be brought up in fair London,
　With one that was his friend.

Away then went the pretty babes,
　Rejoicing at that tide,
Rejoicing with a merry mind
　They should on cock-horse ride.

They prate and prattle pleasantly,
　As they ride on the way,
To those that should their butchers be,
　And work their lives' decay :

So that the pretty speech they had
　Made murderers' hearts relent ;
And they that took the deed to do
　Full sore they did repent.

Yet one of them, more hard of heart,
　Did vow to do his charge,
Because the wretch that hired him
　Had paid him very large.

The other would not agree thereto,
　So here they fell at strife ;
With one another they did fight
　About the children's life.

And he that was of mildest mood
  Did slay the other there,
Within an unfrequented wood,
  While babes did quake for fear.

He took the children by the hand,
  When tears stood in their eye,
And bade them come and go with him,
  And look they did not cry.

And two long miles he led them thus,
  While they for bread complain :
" Stay here," quoth he ; " I'll bring ye bread
  When I do come again."

These pretty babes, with hand in hand,
  Went wandering up and down ;
But never more they saw the man
  Approaching from the town.

Their pretty lips with blackberries
  Were all besmeared and dyed,
And when they saw the darksome night
  They sat them down and cried.

Thus wandered these two pretty babes
  Till death did end their grief,
In one another's arms they died,
  As babes wanting relief.

No burial these pretty babes
    Of any man receives,
Till Robin Redbreast painfully
    Did cover them with leaves.

And now the heavy wrath of God
    Upon their uncle fell;
Yea, fearful fiends did haunt his house, —
    His conscience felt a hell.

His barns were fired, his goods consumed,
　His lands were barren made ;
His cattle died within the field,
　And nothing with him stayed.

And in a voyage to Portugal
　Two of his sons did die ;
And, to conclude, himself was brought
　Unto much misery.

He pawned and mortgaged all his lands
　Ere seven years came about ;
And now, at length, this wicked act
　By this means did come out :

The fellow that did take in hand
　These children for to kill
Was for a robbery judged to die,
　As was God's blessèd will.

Who did confess the very truth
　That is herein expressed :
The uncle died, while he, for debt,
　Did in a prison rest.

OLD CHRISTMAS.

A WORD OF ADVICE TO EXECUTORS.

All ye who be executors made,
   And overseers eke,
Of children that be fatherless,
   And infants mild and meek,

Take you example by this thing,
   And yield to each his right;
Lest God, by such like misery,
   Your wicked deeds requite.

———∘○∵⊛∵○∘———

OLD CHRISTMAS.

———

Now, he who knows old Christmas,
   He knows a carle of worth;
For he is as good a fellow
   As any upon the earth.

He comes warm-cloaked and coated
   And buttoned up to the chin:
And soon as he comes a-nigh the door
   We open and let him in.

We know he will not fail us,
  So we sweep the hearth up clean ;
We set for him the old arm-chair,
  And a cushion whereon to lean.

And with sprigs of holly and ivy
  We make the house look gay,
Just out of old regard to him, —
  For 'twas his ancient way.

He comes with a cordial voice
  That does one good to hear,
He shakes one heartily by the hand,
  As he hath done many a year.

And after the little children
  He asks in a cheerful tone,
Jack, Kate, and little Annie;
  He remembers them every one!

What a fine old fellow he is!
  With his faculties all as clear,
And his heart as warm and light
  As a man in his fortieth year!

What a fine old fellow, in troth!
  No tone of your griping elves,
Who, with plenty of money to spare,
  Think only about themselves.

Not he! for he loveth the children,
  And holiday begs for all;
And comes with his pockets full of gifts
  For the great ones and the small.

And he tells us witty old stories,
  And singeth with might and main;
And we talk of the old man's visit
  Till the day that he comes again.

And all the workhouse children
　　He sets them in a row,
And giveth them rare plum-pudding,
　　And twopence apiece also.

He must be a rich old fellow, —
·　What money he gives away !
There's not a lord in England
　　Could equal him any day !

Good luck unto old Christmas,
　　And long life, let us sing,
For he doth more good unto the poor
　　Than many a crownéd king !

MARY HOWITT.

A VISIT FROM ST. NICHOLAS.

'Twas the night before Christmas, when all through the
　　house
Not a creature was stirring, not even a mouse ;
The stockings were hung by the chimney with care,
In hopes that St. Nicholas soon would be there ;
The children were nestled all snug in their beds,
While visions of sugar-plums danced in their heads ;

And mamma in her kerchief, and I in my cap,
Had just settled our brains for a long winter nap, —
When out on the lawn there arose such a clatter,
I sprang from my bed to see what was the matter.
Away to the window I flew like a flash,
Tore open the shutters and threw up the sash.
The moon, on the breast of the new-fallen snow,
Gave a lustre of midday to objects below ;
When what to my wondering eyes should appear
But a miniature sleigh and eight tiny reindeer,
With a little old driver, so lively and quick,
I knew in a moment it must be St. Nick.
More rapid than eagles his coursers they came,
And he whistled, and shouted, and called them by name :
" Now, Dasher ! now, Dancer ! now, Prancer and Vixen !
On ! Comet, on ! Cupid, on ! Dunder and Blixen ! —
To the top of the porch, to the top of the wall !
Now, dash away, dash away, dash away all ! "
As dry leaves that before the wild hurricane fly,
When they meet with an obstacle, mount to the sky,
So up to the house-top the coursers they flew,
With the sleigh full of toys — and St. Nicholas too.
And then in a twinkling I heard on the roof
The prancing and pawing of each little hoof.
As I drew in my head, and was turning around,
Down the chimney St. Nicholas came with a bound.

He was dressed all in fur from his head to his foot,
And his clothes were all tarnished with ashes and soot,
A bundle of toys he had flung on his back,
And he looked like a peddler just opening his pack.
His eyes, how they twinkle! his dimples, how merry!
His cheeks were like roses, his nose like a cherry;
His droll little mouth was drawn up like a bow,
And the beard on his chin was as white as the snow.
The stump of a pipe he held tight in his teeth,
And the smoke, it encircled his head like a wreath.
He had a broad face and a little round belly
That shook, when he laughed, like a bowl full of jelly.
He was chubby and plump — a right jolly old elf;
And I laughed when I saw him, in spite of myself.
A wink of his eye, and a twist of his head,
Soon gave me to know I had nothing to dread.
He spoke not a word, but went straight to his work,
And filled all the stockings; then turned with a jerk,
And laying his finger aside of his nose,
And giving a nod, up the chimney he rose.
He sprang to his sleigh, to his team gave a whistle,
And away they all flew like the down of a thistle;
But I heard him exclaim, ere he drove out of sight,
"Happy Christmas to all, and to all a good-night!"

C. C. MOORE.

LITTLE MAY.

Have you heard the waters singing,
  Little May,
Where the willows green are bending
  O'er their way?
Do you know how low and sweet,
O'er the pebbles at their feet,
Are the words the waves repeat,
  Night and day?

Have you heard the robins singing,
  Little one,
When the rosy dawn is breaking, —
  When 'tis done?
Have you heard the wooing breeze,
In the blossomed orchard trees,
And the drowsy hum of bees
  In the sun?

All the earth is full of music,
  Little May, —
Bird, and bee, and water singing
  On its way.

Let their silver voices fall
On thy heart with happy call:
" Praise the Lord, who loveth all,"
          Night and day,
          Little May.

                                        MRS. MILLER.

———o○¦○○———

FREDDIE AND THE CHERRY-TREE.

FREDDIE saw some fine ripe cherries
          Hanging on a cherry-tree,
And he said, " You pretty cherries,
          Will you not come down to me? "

" Thank you, kindly," said a cherry;
          " We would rather stay up here;
If we ventured down this morning,
          You would eat us up, I fear."

One, the finest of the cherries,
          Dangled from a slender twig.
" You are beautiful," said Freddie,
          " Red and ripe, and oh, how big ! "

" Catch me," said the cherry, "catch me,
  Little master, if you can."—
" I would catch you soon," said Freddie,
  "If I were a grown-up man."

Freddie jumped, and tried to reach it,
  Standing high upon his toes ;
But the cherry bobbed about,
  And laughed, and tickled Freddie's nose.

" Never mind," said little Freddie,
  " I shall have them when it's right."
But a blackbird whistled boldly,
  " I shall eat them all to-night."

AUNT EFFIE'S RHYMES.

THE TREE.

The Tree's early leaf-buds were bursting their brown :
" Shall I take them away?" said the Frost, sweeping
    down.
          " No, leave them alone
          Till the blossoms have grown,"
Prayed the Tree, while he trembled from rootlet to crown.

The Tree bore his blossoms, and all the birds sung :
" Shall I take them away ? " said the wind, as he swung.
       " No, leave them alone
       Till the berries have grown,"
Said the Tree, while his leaflets quivering hung.

The Tree bore his fruit in the midsummer glow :
Said the girl, " May I gather thy berries now ? "—
       " Yes, all thou canst see :
       Take them ; all are for thee,"
Said the Tree, while he bent down his laden boughs low.

BJÖRNSON.

THE DEATH OF COCK ROBIN AND JENNY WREN.

'Twas a cold autumn morning when Jenny Wren died,
  Cock Robin sat by for to see,
And when all was over he bitterly cried,
  So kind and so loving was he.

He buried her under the little moss-heap
  That lies at the foot of the yew,
And by day and by night he sat near her to weep,
  Till his feathers were wet with the dew.

" O Jenny, I am tired of lingering here,
  Through the dreary, dark days of November,
And I'm thinking of nothing but you, Jenny dear,
  And your loving, fond ways I remember.

" I think how you looked in your little brown suit,
  When you said that you'd always be mine ;
With your fan in your hand, how you glanced at the fruit,
  And said you liked cherries and wine !

" I think of the sweet, merry days of the spring,
  Of the nest that we built both together,
Of the dear little brood nestled under your wing,
  And the joys of the warm summer weather."

And as he lamented, the rain did down pour
  Till his body was wet through and through ;
And he sang, " Dearest Jenny, my sorrows are o'er,
  And I'm coming, my true love, to you."

So he gathered some brown leaves to lay by her side,
  And to pillow his poor, weary head,
And sang, "Jenny, my lost one, my fond one, my bride,"
  Till the gallant Cock Robin fell dead.

                                        GERDA FAY.

RANGER.

A little boat in a cave,
  And a child there fast asleep,
Floating out on a wave,
  Out to the perilous deep, —
Out to the living waters,
  That brightly dance and gleam,
And dart their foam about him,
  To wake him from his dream.

He rubs his pretty eyes,
  He shakes his curly head,
And says, with great surprise,
  " Why, I'm not asleep in bed ! "
The boat is rising and sinking
  Over the sailors' graves ;
And he laughs out, " Isn't it nice,
  Playing see-saw with the waves ? "

Alas ! he little thinks
  Of the grief on the far-off sands,
Where his mother trembles and shrinks,
  And his sister wrings her hands ;
Watching in speechless terror
  The boat and the flaxen head.
Is there no hope of succor ?
  Must they see him drowned or dead ?

They see him living now,
   Living and jumping about;
He stands on the giddy prow,
   With a merry laugh and shout.
Oh! spare him! spare him! spare him!
   Spare him, thou cruel deep!
The child is swept from the prow,
   And the wild waves dance and leap.

They run to the edge of the shore,
　　They stretch out their arms to him ;
Knee-deep they wade, and more ;
　　But alas ! they cannot swim.
Their pretty, pretty darling !
　　His little hat floats by ;
They see his frightened face ;
　　They hear his drowning cry.

Something warm and strong
　　Dashes before them then,
Hairy and curly and strong,
　　And brave as a dozen men ;
Bounding, panting, gasping,
　　Rushing straight as a dart ;
Ready to die in the cause, —
　　A dog with a loyal heart.

He fights with the fighting sea,
　　He grandly wins his prize !
Mother ! he brings it thee
　　With triumph in his eyes.
He brings it thee, O mother !
　　His burden pretty and pale ;
He lays it down at thy feet,
　　And wags his honest old tail.

O dog, so faithful and bold!
　O dog, so tender and true!
You shall wear a collar of gold, —
　And a crown, if you like it, too;
O Ranger! in love and honor
　Your name shall be handed down;
And children's hearts shall beat
　At the tale of your renown.

POEMS FOR A CHILD.

——○○;○;○○——

RANGER'S GRAVE.

He's dead and gone! he's dead and gone!
　And the lime-tree branches wave,
　　And the daisy blows,
　　And the green grass grows,
　　　Upon his grave.

He's dead and gone! he's dead and gone!
　And he sleeps by the flowering lime,
　　Where he loved to lie,
　　When the sun was high,
　　　In summer time.

We've laid him there, where the
blesséd air
Disports with the lovely light,
And raineth showers
Of those sweet flowers,
So silver white.

Where the blackbird sings, and the wild
bee's wings
Make music all day long,
And the cricket at night
(A dusky sprite!)
Takes up the song.

He loved to lie where his wakeful eye
  Could keep me still in sight,
    Whence a word or a sign,
    Or a look of mine,
      Brought him like light.

Nor word nor sign, nor look of mine,
  From under the lime-tree bough,
    With bark and bound,
    And frolic round,
      Shall bring him now.

But he taketh his rest, where he loved best
  In the days of his life to be,
    And that place will not
    Be a common spot
      Of earth to me.

Mrs. Southey.

LOCHINVAR.

Oh, young Lochinvar is come out of the west;
Through all the wide Border his steed was the best,
And save his good broadsword he weapons had none;
He rode all unarmed, and he rode all alone.
So faithful in love, and so dauntless in war,
There never was knight like the young Lochinvar.

He stayed not for brake, and he stopped not for stone,
He swam the Eske river where ford there was none ;
But, ere he alighted at Netherby gate,
The bride had consented, the gallant came late :
For a laggard in love and a dastard in war
Was to wed the fair Ellen of brave Lochinvar.

So boldly he entered the Netherby hall,
Among bridesmen and kinsmen, and brothers and all :
Then spoke the bride's father, his hand on his sword
(For the poor craven bridegroom said never a word),
" Oh, come ye in peace here, or come ye in war,
Or to dance at our bridal, young Lord Lochinvar?"

" I long wooed your daughter, my suit you denied ; —
Love swells like the Solway, but ebbs like its tide ;
And now I am come, with this lost love of mine
To lead but one measure, drink one cup of wine.
There are maidens in Scotland more lovely by far
That would gladly be bride to the young Lochinvar."

The bride kissed the goblet ; the knight took it up :
He quaffed off the wine, and he threw down the cup.
She looked down to blush, and she looked up to sigh,
With a smile on her lips and a tear in her eye.
He took her soft hand ere her mother could bar, —
" Now tread we a measure ! " said young Lochinvar.

So stately his form, and so lovely her face,
That never a hall such a galliard did grace;
While her mother did fret, and her father did fume,
And the bridegroom stood dangling his bonnet and
    plume;
And the bride-maidens whispered, " 'Twere better by far
To have matched our fair cousin with young Lochinvar."

One touch to her hand, and one word in her ear,
When they reached the hall door and the charger stood
    near ;
So light to the croup the fair lady he swung,
So light to the saddle before her he sprung !
" She is won ! we are gone, over bank, bush, and scaur !
They'll have fleet steeds that follow ! " quoth young
    Lochinvar.

There was mounting 'mong Græmes of the Netherby clan ;
Forsters, Fenwicks, and Musgraves, they rode and they
    ran ;
There was racing and chasing on Cannobie Lee ;
But the lost bride of Netherby ne'er did they see.
So daring in love, and so dauntless in war,
Have ye e'er heard of gallant like young Lochinvar ?

SCOTT.

——o-o¦-◦¦-oo———

THE BATTLE OF BLENHEIM.

————

It was a summer's evening,
    Old Kaspar's work was done,
And he before his cottage door
    Was sitting in the sun ;
And by him sported on the green
His little grandchild Wilhelmine.

She saw her brother Peterkin
  Roll something large and round,
Which he, beside the rivulet,
  In playing there, had found.
He came to ask what he had found,
That was so large, and smooth, and round.

Old Kaspar took it from the boy,
  Who stood expectant by ;
And then the old man shook his head,
  And, with a natural sigh,
" 'Tis some poor fellow's skull," said he,
" Who fell in the great victory !

" I find them in the garden,
  For there's many here about ;
And often when I go to plough,
  The ploughshare turns them out ;
For many thousand men," said he,
" Were slain in that great victory ! "

" Now, tell us what 'twas all about,"
  Young Peterkin he cries ;
And little Wilhelmine looks up
  With wonder-waiting eyes ;
" Now tell us all about the war,
And what they killed each other for."

"It was the English," Kaspar cried,
  "Who put the French to rout;
But what they killed each other for
  I could not well make out.
But everybody said," quoth he,
  "That 'twas a famous victory!

" My father lived at Blenheim then,
   Yon little stream hard by :
They burned his dwelling to the ground,
   And he was forced to fly ;
So with his wife and child he fled,
Nor had he where to rest his head.

" With fire and sword the country round
   Was wasted far and wide ;
And many a childing mother then
   And new-born baby died.
But things like that, you know, must be
At every famous victory.

" They say it was a shocking sight
   After the field was won ;
For many thousand bodies here
   Lay rotting in the sun.
But things like that, you know, must be
After a famous victory.

" Great praise the Duke of Marlborough won,
   And our good Prince Eugene." —
" Why, 'twas a very wicked thing ! "
   Said little Wilhelmine.
" Nay, nay, my little girl," quoth he,
" It was a famous victory !

        " And everybody praised the Duke
          Who this great fight did win." —
        " But what good came of it at last?"
          Quoth little Peterkin.
        " Why, that I cannot tell," said he,
        " But 'twas a famous victory!"

                                        SOUTHEY.

                    —⚬⚬⚬⚬⚬—

THE SOLDIER'S DREAM.

Our bugles sang truce — for the night-cloud had lowered,
    And the sentinel stars set their watch in the sky;
And thousands had sunk on the ground overpowered,
    The weary to sleep and the wounded to die.

When reposing that night on my pallet of straw,
    By the wolf-scaring fagot that guarded the slain,
At the dead of the night a sweet vision I saw,
    And thrice ere the morning I dreamt it again.

Methought from the battle-field's dreadful array,
    Far, far I had roamed on a desolate track:
'Twas autumn, and sunshine arose on the way
    To the home of my fathers, that welcomed me back.

I flew to the pleasant fields traversed so oft
    In life's morning march, when my bosom was young;
I heard my own mountain goats bleating aloft,
    And knew the sweet strain that the corn-reapers sung.

Then pledged we the wine-cup, and fondly I swore,
    From my home and my weeping friends never to part;
My little ones kissed me a thousand times o'er,
    And my wife sobbed aloud in her fulness of heart,

"Stay, stay with us, — rest, thou art weary and worn;"
    And fain was their war-broken soldier to stay;
But sorrow returned with the dawning of morn,
    And the voice in my dreaming ear melted away.

CAMPBELL.

THE BURIAL OF SIR JOHN MOORE.

Not a drum was heard, not a funeral note,
    As his corse to the ramparts we hurried;
Not a soldier discharged his farewell shot
    O'er the grave where our hero we buried.

We buried him darkly at dead of night,
　The sods with our bayonets turning,
By the struggling moonbeams' misty light,
　And the lantern dimly burning.

No useless coffin enclosed his breast,
　Nor in sheet or in shroud we wound him;
But he lay like a warrior taking his rest,
　With his martial cloak around him.

Few and short were the prayers we said,
 And we spoke not a word of sorrow ;
But we steadfastly gazed on the face of the dead,
 And we bitterly thought of the morrow.

We thought, as we hollowed his narrow bed,
 And smoothed down his lonely pillow,
That the foe and the stranger would tread o'er his head,
 And we far away on the billow.

Lightly they'll talk of the spirit that's gone,
 And o'er his cold ashes upbraid him ;
But little he'll reck, if they let him sleep on
 In the grave where a Briton has laid him.

But half of our heavy task was done,
 When the clock struck the hour for retiring ;
And we heard the distant and random gun
 That the foe was sullenly firing.

Slowly and sadly we laid him down,
 From the field of his fame fresh and gory ;
We carved not a line, and we raised not a stone,
 But we left him alone with his glory.

        WOLFE.

OLD IRONSIDES.

Ay, tear her tattered ensign down !
  Long has it waved on high,
And many an eye has danced to see
  That banner in the sky ;
Beneath it rung the battle shout,
  And burst the cannon's roar :
The meteor of the ocean air
  Shall sweep the clouds no more.

Her deck, once red with heroes' blood,
  Where knelt the vanquished foe,
When winds were hurrying o'er the flood,
  And waves were white below,
No more shall feel the victor's tread,
  Or know the conquered knee ; —
The harpies of the shore shall pluck
  The eagle of the sea !

Oh, better that her shattered hulk
  Should sink beneath the wave ;
Her thunders shook the mighty deep,
  And there should be her grave ;

Nail to the mast her holy flag,
  Set every threadbare sail,
And give her to the god of storms,
  The lightning and the gale !

HOLMES.

SWEET HOME.

'Mid pleasures and palaces though we may roam,
Be it ever so humble, there's no place like home !
A charm from the skies seems to hallow us here,
Which, seek through the world, is ne'er met with else-
　　　　　where.
　　　Home, home, sweet home !
　　　There's no place like home !

An exile from home, splendor dazzles in vain !
Oh, give me my lowly thatched cottage again !
The birds singing gayly that came at my call ; —
Oh, give me sweet peace of mind, dearer than all !
　　　Home, home, sweet home !
　　　There's no place like home !

　　　　　　　　　　　　　　　PAYNE.

THE TRAVELLER'S RETURN.

Sweet to the morning traveller
  The song amid the sky,
Where, twinkling in the dewy light,
  The skylark soars on high.

And cheering to the traveller
  The gales that round him play,
When faint and heavily he drags
  Along his noontide way.

And when beneath the unclouded sun
  Full wearily toils he,
The flowing water makes to him
  A soothing melody.

And when the evening light decays,
  And all is calm around,
There is sweet music to his ear
  In the distant sheep-bell's sound.

But, oh! of all delightful sounds
  Of evening or of morn,
The sweetest is the voice of love
  That welcomes his return.

                SOUTHEY.

THE HOMES OF ENGLAND.

The stately Homes of England!
  How beautiful they stand,
Amidst their tall, ancestral trees,
  O'er all the pleasant land!
The deer across their greensward bound,
  Through shade and sunny gleam,
And the swan glides past them with the sound
  Of some rejoicing stream.

The merry Homes of England!
  Around their hearths by night,
What gladsome looks of household love
  Meet in the ruddy light!
There woman's voice flows forth in song,
  Or childish tale is told,
Or lips move tunefully along
  Some glorious page of old.

The blessed Homes of England!
  How softly on their bowers
Is laid the holy quietness
  That breathes from Sabbath hours!

Solemn, yet sweet, the church bells' chime
   Floats through their woods at morn ;
All other sounds, in that still time,
   Of breeze and leaf are born.

The cottage Homes of England !
   By thousands on her plains
They're smiling o'er the silv'ry brooks,
   And round the hamlet fanes.
Through glowing orchards forth they peep,
   Each from its nook of leaves ;
And fearless there the lowly sleep,
   As the bird beneath their eaves.

The free, fair Homes of England !
   Long, long, in hut and hall,
May hearts of native proof be reared
   To guard each hallowed wall !
And green forever be the groves,
   And bright the flowery sod,
Where first the child's glad spirit loves
   Its country and its God !

                    MRS. HEMANS.

LORD ULLIN'S DAUGHTER.

A chieftain to the Highlands bound
  Cries, "Boatman, do not tarry!
And I'll give thee a silver pound
  To row us o'er the ferry."

"Now, who be ye would cross Lochgyle,
  This dark and stormy water?" —
"Oh, I am chief of Ulva's isle,
  And this, Lord Ullin's daughter.

" And fast before her father's men
   Three days we've fled together ;
For, should he find us in the glen,
   My blood would stain the heather.

" His horsemen hard behind us ride ;
   Should they our steps discover,
Then who would cheer my bonny bride
   When they have slain her lover?"

Out spoke the hardy island wight,
   " I'll go, my chief — I'm ready : —
It is not for your silver bright,
   But for your winsome lady ;

" And by my word, the bonny bird
   In danger shall not tarry ;
So, though the waves are raging white,
   I'll row you o'er the ferry."

By this the storm grew loud apace,
   The water-wraith was shrieking,
And in the scowl of heaven each face
   Grew dark as they were speaking.

But still as wilder blew the wind,
   And as the night grew drearer,
Adown the glen rode arméd men,
   Their tramping sounded nearer.

" Oh, haste thee, haste ! " the lady cries ;
   " Though tempests round us gather ;
I'll meet the raging of the skies,
   But not an angry father."

The boat has left a stormy land,
   A stormy sea before her, —
When, oh ! too strong for human hand,
   The tempest gathered o'er her.

And still they rowed amidst the roar
   Of waters fast prevailing ;
Lord Ullin reached that fatal shore, —
   His wrath was changed to wailing.

For sore dismayed, through storm and shade,
   His child he did discover :
One lovely hand she stretched for aid,
   And one was round her lover.

" Come back ! come back ! " he cried in grief,
   " Across this stormy water ;
And I'll forgive your Highland chief,
   My daughter ! — O my daughter ! "

'Twas vain : the loud waves lashed the shore,
   Return or aid preventing ;
The waters wild went o'er his child,
   And he was left lamenting.

                                        CAMPBELL.

TO MY MOTHER.

And canst thou, mother, for a moment think
   That we, thy children, when old age shall shed
   Its blanching honors on thy weary head,
Could from our best of duties ever shrink?
Sooner the sun from his bright sphere shall sink,
   Than we ungrateful leave thee in that day,
   To pine in solitude thy life away,
Or shun thee tottering on the grave's cold brink.
Banish the thought! — where'er our steps may roam,
   O'er smiling plains, or wastes without a tree,
   Still will fond memory point our hearts to thee,
And paint the pleasures of thy peaceful home;
While duty bids us all thy griefs assuage,
And smooth the pillow of thy sinking age.

KIRKE WHITE.

THE THREE FRIENDS.

Three young girls in friendship met, —
Mary, Martha, Margaret.

Margaret was tall and fair,
Martha shorter by a hair ;

If the first excelled in feature,
The other's grace and ease were greater;
Mary, though to rival loth,
In their best gifts equalled both.
They a due proportion kept;
Martha mourned if Margaret wept;
Margaret joyed when any good
She of Martha understood;
And in sympathy for either
Mary was outdone by neither.

Thus far, for a happy space,
All three ran an even race,
A most constant friendship proving,
Equally beloved and loving;
All their wishes, joys, the same;
Sisters only not in name.

CHARLES LAMB.

ABOU BEN ADHEM AND THE ANGEL.

Abou Ben Adhem (may his tribe increase!)
Awoke one night from a deep dream of peace,
And saw, within the moonlight in his room,
Making it rich, like a lily in bloom,
An angel writing in a book of gold.
Exceeding peace had made Ben Adhem bold,
And to the Presence in the room he said,
" What writest thou?"   The vision raised its head,
And with a look made all of sweet accord
Answered, " The names of those who love the Lord."
" And is mine one?" said Abou.   " Nay, not so,"
Replied the angel.   Abou spoke more low,
But cheerly still, and said, " I pray thee, then,
Write me as one that loves his fellow-men."

The angel wrote and vanished.   The next night
It came again with a great wakening light,
And showed the names whom love of God had blest,
And, lo! Ben Adhem's name led all the rest.

LEIGH HUNT.

THE HAUNTED SPRING.

Gayly through the mountain glen
  The hunter's horn did ring,
    As the milk-white doe
    Escaped his bow,
  Down by the haunted spring.
In vain his silver horn he wound, —
  'Twas echo answering back ;
For neither groom nor baying hound
  Was on the hunter's track :
In vain he sought the milk-white doe
That made him stray and 'scaped his bow,
For, save himself, no living thing
Was by the silent haunted spring.

The purple heath-bells, blooming fair,
  Their fragrance round did fling,
    As the hunter lay,
    At close of day,
  Down by the haunted spring.
A lady fair, in robe of white,
  To greet the hunter came ;
She kissed a cup with jewels bright,
  And pledged him by his name.

" O lady fair," the hunter cried,
" Be thou my love, my blooming
      bride, --
A bride that well might grace a king !
Fair lady of the haunted spring."

In the fountain clear she stooped,
   And forth she drew a ring ;
     And that loved knight
      His faith did plight
   Down by the haunted spring.

But since that day his chase did stray,
  The hunter ne'er was seen,
And legends tell he now doth dwell
  Within the hills so green ;
But still the milk-white doe appears.
And wakes the peasants' evening fears,
While distant bugles faintly ring
Around the lonely haunted spring.

LOVER.

<hr />

A FAIRY'S SONG.

Over hill, over dale,
  Through bush, through briar,
Over park, over pale,
  Through flood, through fire,
I do wander everywhere,
Swifter than the moon's sphere ;
And I serve the Fairy Queen,
To dew her orbs upon the green.
The cowslips tall her pensioners be ;
In their gold coats spots you see, —
These be rubies, fairy favors,
In those freckles live their savors.
I must go seek some dew-drops here,
And hang a pearl in every cowslip's ear.

SHAKESPEARE.

NOSE AND EYES.

Between Nose and Eyes a strange contest arose ;
    The spectacles set them unhappily wrong ;
The point in dispute was, as all the world knows,
    To which the said spectacles ought to belong.

So the Tongue was the lawyer, and argued the cause
    With a great deal of skill, and a wig full of learning ;
While Chief-justice Ear sat to balance the laws,
    So famed for his talent in nicely discerning.

" In behalf of the Nose, it will quickly appear,
    And your lordship," he said, " will undoubtedly find,
That the Nose has had spectacles always in wear, —
    Which amounts to possession time out of mind."

Then holding the spectacles up to the court, —
    " Your lordship observes they are made with a straddle
As wide as the ridge of the Nose is ; in short,
    Designed to sit close to it, just like a saddle.

" Again, would your lordship a moment suppose
    ('Tis a case that has happened, and may be again)
That the visage or countenance had not a Nose,
    Pray who would or who could wear spectacles then ?

" On the whole it appears, and my argument shows,
  With a reasoning the court will never condemn,
That the spectacles plainly were made for the Nose,
  And the Nose was as plainly intended for them."

Then, shifting his side, as a lawyer knows how,
  He pleaded again in behalf of the Eyes;
But what were his arguments few people know,
  For the court did not think they were equally wise.

So his lordship decreed, with a grave, solemn tone,
  Decisive and clear, without one *if* or *but*, —
That whenever the Nose put his spectacles on,
  By daylight or candle-light, Eyes should be shut.

COWPER.

THE WIND IN A FROLIC.

The wind one morning sprang up from sleep,
Saying, " Now for a frolic ! now for a leap !
Now for a madcap galloping chase !
I'll make a commotion in every place ! "
So it swept with a bustle right through a great town,
Creaking the signs, and scattering down
Shutters, and whisking, with merciless squalls,
Old women's bonnets and gingerbread stalls.
There never was heard a much lustier shout,
As the apples and oranges tumbled about ;
And the urchins, that stand with their thievish eyes
Forever on watch, ran off each with a prize.
 Then away to the fields it went blustering and
  humming,
And the cattle all wondered whatever was coming.
It plucked by their tails the grave, matronly cows,
And tossed the colts' manes all about their brows,
Till, offended at such a familiar salute,
They all turned their backs and stood silently mute.
So on it went, capering and playing its pranks ;
Whistling with reeds on the broad river banks ;

Puffing the birds, as they sat on the spray,
Or the traveller grave on the king's highway.
It was not too nice to bustle the bags
Of the beggar, and flutter his dirty rags.
'Twas so bold that it feared not to play its joke
With the doctor's wig, and the gentleman's cloak.
Through the forest it roared, and cried gayly, " Now,
You sturdy old oaks, I'll make you bow ! "
And it made them bow without more ado,
Or it cracked their great branches through and through.
   Then it rushed like a monster o'er cottage and farm,
Striking their inmates with sudden alarm ;
And they ran out like bees in a midsummer swarm.
There were dames with their kerchiefs tied over their
      caps,
To see if their poultry were free from mishaps ;
The turkeys they gobbled, the geese screamed aloud,
And the hens crept to roost in a terrified crowd ;
There was rearing of ladders, and logs laying on,
Where the thatch from the roof threatened soon to be
      gone.
   But the wind had passed on, and had met in a lane
With a school-boy, who panted and struggled in vain,
For it tossed him, and twirled him, then passed, and he
      stood
With his hat in a pool, and his shoe in the mud.

                                    WILLIAM HOWITT.

THE INCHCAPE ROCK.

No stir in the air, no stir in the sea :
The ship was still as she could be ;
Her sails from heaven received no motion,
Her keel was steady in the ocean.

Without either sign or sound of their shock
The waves flowed over the Inchcape Rock ;
So little they rose, so little they fell,
They did not move the Inchcape Bell.

The Abbot of Aberbrothok
Had placed that bell on the Inchcape Rock ;
On a buoy in the storm it floated and swung,
And over the waves its warning rung.

When the rock was hid by the surge's swell,
The mariners heard the warning bell ;
And then they knew the perilous rock,
And blessed the Abbot of Aberbrothok.

The sun in heaven was shining gay,
All things were joyful on that day ;
The sea-birds screamed as they wheeled round,
And there was joyaunce in their sound.

The buoy of the Inchcape Bell was seen
A darker speck on the ocean green ;
Sir Ralph the Rover walked his deck,
And he fixed his eyes on the darker speck.

He felt the cheering power of spring,
It made him whistle, it made him sing ;
His heart was mirthful to excess, —
But the Rover's mirth was wickedness.

His eye was on the Inchcape float :
Quoth he, " My men, put out the boat,
And row me to the Inchcape Rock,
And I'll plague the Abbot of Aberbrothok."

The boat is lowered, the boatmen row,
And to the Inchcape Rock they go ;
Sir Ralph bent over from the boat,
And he cut the bell from the Inchcape float.

Down sank the bell with a gurgling sound,
The bubbles rose and burst around ;
Quoth Sir Ralph, " The next who comes to
    the Rock
Won't bless the Abbot of Aberbrothok."

Sir Ralph the Rover sailed away,
He scoured the seas for many a day ;
And now, grown rich with plundered store,
He steers his course for Scotland's shore.

So thick a haze o'erspreads the sky
They cannot see the sun on high ;
The wind hath blown a gale all day,
At evening it hath died away.

On the deck the Rover takes his stand ;
So dark it is they see no land.
Quoth Sir Ralph, " It will be lighter soon,
For there is the dawn of the rising moon."

" Canst hear," said one, " the breakers roar ? —
For methinks we should be near the shore."
" Now where we are I cannot tell,
But I wish I could hear the Inchcape Bell."

They hear no sound ; the swell is strong ;
Though the wind hath fallen they drift along,
Till the vessel strikes with a shivering shock : —
" O Christ ! it is the Inchcape Rock ! "

Sir Ralph the Rover tore his hair,
And beat his breast in his despair ;
The waves rush in on every side,
And the ship sinks down beneath the tide.

SOUTHEY.

THE THREE BELLS.

Beneath the low-hung night cloud
  That raked her splintering mast
The good ship settled slowly,
  The cruel leak gained fast.

Over the awful ocean
  Her signal guns pealed out.
Dear God ! was that thy answer
  From the horror round about?

A voice came down the wild wind,
  " Ho ! ship ahoy ! " its cry ;
" Our stout Three Bells of Glasgow
  Shall lay till daylight by ! "

Hour after hour crept slowly,
  Yet on the heaving swells
Tossed up and down the ship-lights,
  The lights of the Three Bells !

And ship to ship made signals,
  Man answered back to man,
While oft, to cheer and hearten,
  The Three Bells nearer ran ;

And the captain from her taffrail
  Sent down his hopeful cry;
" Take heart! Hold on!" he shouted,
  " The Three Bells shall lay by!"

All night across the waters
  The tossing lights shone clear;
All night from reeling taffrail
  The Three Bells sent her cheer.

And when the dreary watches
　Of storm and darkness passed,
Just as the wreck lurched under,
　All souls were saved at last.

Sail on, Three Bells, forever,
　In grateful memory sail!
Ring on, Three Bells of rescue,
　Above the wave and gale!

Type of the Love eternal,
　Repeat the Master's cry,
As tossing through our darkness
　The lights of God draw nigh!

WHITTIER.

A, B, C.

By Alpine lake, 'neath shady rock,
The herd-boy knelt beside his flock,
And softly told, with pious air,
His alphabet as evening prayer.

Unseen, his pastor lingered near :
" My child, what means the sound I hear ? " —
" May I not in the worship share,
And raise to Heaven my evening prayer ?

" Where'er the hills and valleys blend,
The sounds of prayer and praise ascend." —
" My child, a prayer yours cannot be :
You've only said your A, B, C."

" I have no better way to pray, —
All that I know to God I say :
I tell the letters on my knees ;
He makes the words himself to please."

POSIES FOR CHILDREN.

CHILD AND THE ANGELS.

The Sabbath's sun was setting low,
　Amidst the clouds at even ;
" Our Father," breathed a voice be-
　　low, —
　" Our Father, who art in heaven."

Beyond the earth, beyond the clouds,
　Those infant words were given ;
" Our Father," angels sang aloud —
　" Father, who art in heaven."

" Thy kingdom come," still from the ground,
　That childlike voice did pray ;
" Thy kingdom come," God's hosts resound,
　Far up the starry way.

" Thy will be done," with little tongue,
  That lisping love implores ;
" Thy will be done," the angelic throng
  Sing from the heavenly shores.

" Forever," still those lips repeat
  Their closing evening prayer ;
" Forever," floats in music sweet,
  High midst the angels there.

C. SWAIN.

LORD, TEACH A LITTLE CHILD.

Lord, teach a little child to pray,
  And, oh, accept my prayer.
Thou hearest all the words I say,
  For Thou art everywhere.

A little sparrow cannot fall
  Unnoticed, Lord, by Thee ;
And though I am so young and small,
  Thou carest still for me.

Teach me to do whate'er is right,
  And when I sin, forgive ;
And make it still my chief delight
  To love Thee while I live.

SLEEP, BABY, SLEEP.

Sleep, baby, sleep !
Thy father watches the sheep ;
Thy mother is shaking the dreamland tree.
And aown comes a little dream on thee.
Sleep, baby, sleep !

Sleep, baby, sleep !
The large stars are the sheep ;
The little stars are the lambs, I guess ;
And the gentle moon is the shepherdess.
Sleep, baby, sleep !

Sleep, baby, sleep !
Our Saviour loves His sheep :
He is the Lamb of God on high,
Who for our sakes came down to die.
Sleep, baby, sleep !

FROM THE GERMAN.

THE LITTLE DREAMER.

A little boy was dreaming,
  Upon his nurse's lap,
That the pins fell out of all the stars,
  And the stars fell into his cap.

So, when his dream was over,
  What should that little boy do?
Why, he went and looked inside his cap,
  And found it wasn't true.

NURSERY NONSENSE.

THE LITTLE BROTHER.

Little brother in a cot,
    Baby, baby !
Shall he have a pleasant lot? —
    Maybe, maybe !

Little brother in a nap,
    Baby, baby !
Bless his tiny little cap,
    Noise far away be !

With a rattle in his hand,
    Baby, baby !
Dreaming, — who can understand
    Dreams like this, what they be?

When he wakes, kiss him twice,
    Then talk and gay be ;
Little cheeks, soft and nice,
    Baby, baby !

LILLIPUT LEVEE.

COCK-A-DOODLE-DOO.

A little boy got out of bed, —
  'Twas only six o'clock, —
And out of window poked his head,
  And spied a crowing cock.

The little boy said, " Mr. Bird,
  Pray tell me who are you?"
And all the answer that he heard
  Was, " Cock-a-doodle-do !"

" What would you think, if you were me,"
  He said, " and I were you?"
But still that bird provokingly
  Cried, " Cock-a-doodle-do !"

" How many times, you stupid head,
  Goes three in twenty-two?"
That old bird winked one eye, and said
  Just " Cock-a-doodle-do !"

He slammed the window down again,
  When up that old bird flew ;
And, pecking at the window-pane,
  Cried, " Cock-a-doodle-doodle-doodle-do !"

Nursery Nonsense.

A little Girls Letter.

Dear Grandma, I will try to write
  A very little letter:
If I don't spell the words all right,
  Why, next time I'll do better.

My little rabbit is alive,
  And likes his milk and clover;
He likes to see me very much,
  But is afraid of Rover.

I've got a dove, as white as snow,
   I call her "Polly Feather;"
She flies and hops about the yard
   In every kind of weather.

I think she likes to see it rain,
   For then she smooths her jacket;
And seems to be so proud and vain,
   The turkeys make a racket.

The hens are picking off the grass
   And singing very loudly;
While our old peacock struts about
   And shows his colors proudly.

I guess I'll close my letter now,
   I've nothing more to tell;
Please answer soon, and come to see
   Your loving little Nell!

                   WISCONSIN FARMER.

A LITTLE BROWN BIRD.

A little brown bird sat on a stone;
   The sun shone thereon, but he was alone.
"O pretty bird, do you not weary
   Of this gay summer so long and dreary?"

The little bird opened his bright black eyes,
   And looked at me with great surprise ;
Then his joyous song broke forth, to say,
   " Weary of what ?   I can sing all day."

Posies for Children.

———o∘⦂⦿⦂∘o———

EGGS AND BIRDS.

" Where is the little lark's nest,
   My father showed to me ?
And where the pretty lark's eggs ? "
   Said master Lori Lee.
At last he found the lark's nest,
   But eggs were none to see.

" Why are you looking down there ? "
   Sang two young larks on high ;
" We've broke the shells that held us,
   And found a nest on high."
And the happy birds went singing
   Far up the morning sky.

Lilliput Levee.

LITTLE BIRDIE.

What does little birdie say,
In her nest, at peep of day?
" Let me fly," says little birdie,
  " Mother, let me fly away." —
" Birdie, rest a little longer,
Till the little wings are stronger."
So she rests a little longer,
  Then she flies away.

What does little baby say,
In her bed, at peep of day?
Baby says, like little birdie,
  " Let me rise and fly away." —
" Baby, sleep a little longer,
Till the little limbs are stronger.
If she sleeps a little longer,
  Baby, too, shall fly away."

TENNYSON.

THE TURTLE DOVE'S NEST.

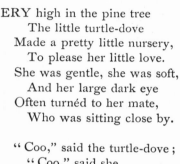

VERY high in the pine tree
    The little turtle-dove
Made a pretty little nursery,
    To please her little love.
She was gentle, she was soft,
    And her large dark eye
Often turnéd to her mate,
    Who was sitting close by.

" Coo," said the turtle-dove ;
    " Coo," said she.
" Oh, I love thee," said the turtle-dove ;
    " And *I* love *thee*."
In the long shady branches
    Of the dark pine tree,
How happy were the doves
    In their little nursery !

The young turtle-doves
    Never quarrelled in the nest,
For they dearly loved each other,
    Though they loved their mother best ;

" Coo," said the little doves ;
  " Coo," said she.
And they played together kindly
  In the dark pine tree.

In this nursery of yours,
  Little sister, little brother,
Like the turtle-dove's nest —
  Do you love one another?
Are you kind, are you gentle,
  As children ought to be?
Then the happiest of nests
  Is your own nursery.

AUNT EFFIE'S RHYMES.

————∘∘⊶⊷∘∘————

DAME DUCK'S FIRST LECTURE ON EDUCATION.

Old Mother Duck has hatched a brood
  Of ducklings, small and callow :
Their little wings are short, their down
  Is mottled gray and yellow.

There is a quiet little stream,
  That runs into the moat,
Where tall green sedges spread their leaves,
  And water-lilies float.

Close by the margin of the brook
  The old duck made her nest
Of straw, and leaves, and withered grass,
  And down from her own breast.

And there she sat for four long weeks,
  In rainy days and fine,
Until the ducklings all came out —
  Four, five, six, seven, eight, nine!

One peeped out from beneath her wing,
  One scrambled on her back;
" That's very rude," said old Dame Duck.
  " Get off! quack, quack, quack, quack!"

" 'Tis close," said Dame Duck, shoving out
  The egg-shells with her bill;
" Besides, it never suits young ducks
  To keep them sitting still."

So, rising from her nest, she said,
  " Now, children, look at me:
A well-bred duck should waddle so,
  From side to side — d'ye see?"

" Yes," said the little ones, and then
   She went on to explain :
" A well-bred duck turns in its toes
   As I do — try again."

' Yes," said the ducklings, waddling on ;
   " That's better," said their mother ;
" But well-bred ducks walk in a row,
   Straight — one behind another."

" Yes," said the little ducks again,
   All waddling in a row ;
" Now to the pond," said old Dame Duck —
   Splash, splash ! and in they go.

" Let me swim first," said old Dame Duck,
   " To this side, now to that ;
There, snap at those great brown-winged flies,
   They make young ducklings fat.

" Now when you reach the poultry-yard,
   The hen-wife, Molly Head,
Will feed you, with the other fowls,
   On bran and mashed-up bread ;

" The hens will peck and fight, but mind,
   I hope that all of you
Will gobble up the food as fast
   As well-bred ducks should do.

" You'd better get into the dish,
  Unless it is too small ;
In that case I should use my foot,
  And overturn it all."

The ducklings did as they were bid,
  And found the plan so good,
That from that day the other fowls
  Got hardly any food.

AUNT EFFIE'S RHYMES.

————oo°○°oo————

WAY TO BE HAPPY.

How pleasant it is at the end of the day
  No follies to have to repent ;
But reflect on the past, and be able to say
  That my time has been properly spent.

When I've done all my business with patience and care,
  And been good, and obliging, and kind,
I lie on my pillow and sleep away there,
  With a happy and peaceable mind.

But instead of all this, if it must be confessed
  That I careless and idle have been,
I lie down as usual, and go to my rest,
  But feel discontented within.

Then, as I don't like all the trouble I've had,
   In future I'll try to prevent it;
For I never am naughty without being sad,
   Or good without being contented.

JANE TAYLOR.

THE STRANGE LITTLE BOY.

Here is a little boy,
   Look at him well:
Think if you know him;
   If you do, tell.
I will describe him,
   That you may see
If he's a stranger
   To you and to me.

He has two hands
   That can manage a top,
And climb a tall chestnut
   To make the nuts drop.
They're just full of business,
   With ball, hoop, and swing;
Yet are never too busy
   To do a kind thing.

He has two feet
That can run up and down
Over the country
And all about town.

I should think they'd be tired, —
They never are still ;
But they're ready to run for you
Whither you will.

He has two eyes,
    Always busy and bright,
And looking at something
    From morning till night.
They help him at work,
    They help him at play,
And the sweet words of Jesus
    They read every day.

He has two ears :
    Oh, how well he can hear
The birds as they sing,
    And the boys as they cheer !
They are out on the Common,
    And for him they call ;
But one word from his mother
    He hears first of all.

He has a tongue
    That moves like a sprite :
It begins in the morning
    As soon as the light.
It's the best little tongue
    You can anywhere find,
For it always speaks truth,
    And it always is kind.

POSIES FOR CHILDREN.

MY JESSIE.

My Jessie lives beyond the town,
Just where the moorland, bare and brown,
    Looks over to the sea:
A little maid of lowly birth,
But, oh! of all the girls on earth,
    The dearest girl to me!

Few summers hath she known : her eyes
Are bluer than the summer skies,
   And brimming o'er with fun ;
Her hair is like a golden crown ;
Her little hands are sadly brown ;
   Her cheek tells of the sun.

But could you see her come and go,
In summer shine and winter snow,
   As I do, day by day ;
Now rising like the lark at morn ;
Like Ruth, now gleaming in the corn ;
   Now busy in the hay ;

Now racing like a greyhound fleet
Along the glist'ning sands, with feet
   Like snow so white and bare ;
All beauty, health, enjoyment, mirth,
You'd say no queen on all the earth
   Was ever half so fair !

Mrs. Edwards.

LITTLE LAMB.

Little lamb, who made thee?
Dost thou know who made thee,
Gave thee life, and made thee feed
By the stream and o'er the mead?
Gave thee clothing of delight, —
Softest clothing, woolly, bright?
Gave thee such a tender voice,
Making all the vales rejoice?
Little lamb, who made thee?
Dost thou know who made thee?

Little lamb, I'll tell thee;
Little lamb, I'll tell thee:
He is calléd by thy name,
For He calls Himself a lamb.
He is meek, and He is mild;
He became a little child:
I a child, and thou a lamb,
We are calléd by His name.
Little lamb, God bless thee!
Little lamb, God bless thee!

BLAKE.

THE NEW MOON.

Dear mother, how pretty
The moon looks to-night!
She was never so cunning before;

The two little horns
Are so sharp and so bright,
I hope she'll not grow any more.

If I were up there,
With you and my friends,
I'd rock in it nicely, you'd see;
I'd sit in the middle
And hold by both ends;
Oh, what a bright cradle 'twould be!

I would call to the stars
To keep out of the way,
Lest we should rock over their toes;
And then I would rock
Till the dawn of the day,
And see where the pretty moon goes.

And there we would stay
In the beautiful skies,
And through the bright clouds we would roam;
We would see the sun set,
And see the sun rise,
And in the next rainbow come home.

MRS. FOLLEN.

THE BUSY BEE.

How doth the little busy bee
   Improve each shining hour,
And gather honey all the day
   From every opening flower !

How skilfully she builds her cell !
   How neat she spreads the wax !
And labors hard to store it well
   With the sweet food she makes.

In works of labor or of skill
   I would be busy too ;
For Satan finds some mischief still
   For idle hands to do.

In books, or work, or healthful play,
   Let my first years be past ;
That I may give for every day
   Some good account at last.

WATTS.

THE ANT.

These emmets, how little they are in our eyes!
We tread them to dust, and a troop of them dies,
    Without our regard or concern ;
Yet as wise as we are, if sent to their school,
There's many a sluggard and many a fool
    Some lessons of wisdom might learn.

They don't wear their time out in sleeping or play,
But gather up corn on a sunshiny day,
    And for winter they lay up their stores ;
They manage their work in such regular forms,
One would think they foresaw all the frosts and the
        storms,
    And so brought their food within doors.

But I have less sense than a poor creeping ant,
If I take not due care for the things I shall want,
    Nor provide against dangers in time ;
When death and old age shall stare in my face,
What a wretch shall I be in the end of my days,
    If I trifle away all their prime !

Now, now while my strength and my youth are in bloom,
Let me think what shall save me when sickness shall
      come,
    And pray that my sins be forgiven ;
Let me read in good books, and believe and obey,
That when death turns me out of this cottage of clay,
    I may dwell in a palace in heaven.

WATTS.

TO A BUTTERFLY.

'VE watched you now a full half-hour,
    Self-poised upon that yellow flower !
    And, little butterfly, indeed,
    I know not if you sleep or feed.

How motionless ! — not frozen seas
    More motionless ; and then,
What joy awaits you when the breeze
Hath found you out among the trees,
    And calls you forth again !

This plot of orchard ground is ours,
My trees they are, my sister's flowers ;
Here rest your wings when they are weary,
Here lodge as in a sanctuary !

Come to us often, fear no wrong ;
  Sit near us on the bough !
We'll talk of sunshine and of song,
And summer days when we were young ;
Sweet childish days, that were as long
  As twenty days are now.

WORDSWORTH.

————∘₀⁚◉⁚₀∘————

THE PRISONER TO A ROBIN WHO CAME TO HIS WINDOW.

———

Welcome ! welcome, little stranger !
  Welcome to my lone retreat !
Here secure from every danger,
  Hop about, and chirp, and eat.
    Robin ! how I envy thee,
    Happy child of liberty !

Hunger never shall distress thee
  While my meals one crumb afford ;
Colds and cramps shall ne'er oppress thee,
  Come and share my humble board ;
    Robin, come and live with me ;
    Live, yet still at liberty.

Soon shall spring, with smiles and blushes,
  Steal upon the blooming year ;
Then, amid the verdant bushes,
   Thy sweet song shall warble clear ;
    Then shall I, too, joined with thee,
    Taste the sweets of liberty.

Liberty ! thou brightest treasure
  In the crown of earthly joys !
Source of gladness ! soul of pleasure !
   All delights besides are toys :
    None but prisoners like me
    Know the worth of liberty.

JAMES MONTGOMERY.

TIME.

———

" Sixty seconds make a minute,
   Sixty minutes make an hour ; "
If I were a little linnet,
   Hopping in her leafy bower,
Then I should not have to sing it :
" Sixty seconds make a minute."

" Twenty-four hours make one day,
   Seven days will make a week : "
And while we all at marbles play,
   Or run at cunning " hide and seek,"
Or in the garden gather flowers,
We'll tell the time that makes the hours.

In every month the weeks are four,
   And twelve whole months will make a year ;
Now I must say it o'er and o'er,
   Or else it never will be clear ;
So once again I will begin it :
" Sixty seconds make a minute."

MABEL ON MIDSUMMER DAY.

A STORY OF THE OLDEN TIME.

PART I.

" Arise, my maiden, Mabel,"
  The mother said ; " arise, •
For the golden sun of midsummer
  Is shining in the skies.

" Arise, my little maiden,
  For thou must speed away,
To wait upon thy grandmother
  This livelong summer day.

" And thou must carry with thee
  This wheaten cake so fine,
This new-made pat of butter,
  This little flask of wine.

" And tell the dear old body,
  This day I cannot come,
For the good man went out yester-morn,
  And he is not come home.

"And more than this, poor Amy
Upon my knee doth lie;
I fear me, with this fever-pain
The little child will die!

"And thou canst help thy grandmother:
The table thou canst spread;
Canst feed the little dog and bird;
And thou canst make her bed.

"And thou canst fetch the water
From the lady-well hard by;
And thou canst gather from the wood
The fagots brown and dry;

" Canst go down to the lonesome glen,
　To milk the mother-ewe ;
This is the work, my Mabel,
　That thou wilt have to do.

" But listen now, my Mabel,
　This is midsummer day,
When all the fairy people
　From elf-land come away.

" And when thou'rt in the lonesome glen,
　Keep by the running burn,
And do not pluck the strawberry-flower,
　Nor break the lady-fern.

" But think not of the fairy folk,
　Lest mischief should befall ;
Think only of poor Amy,
　And how thou lov'st us all.

" Yet keep good heart, my Mabel,
　If thou the fairies see,
And give them kindly answer
　If they should speak to thee.

" And when into the fir-wood
　Thou goest for fagots brown,
Do not, like idle children,
　Go wandering up and down.

" But fill thy little apron,
    My child, with earnest speed ;
And that thou break no living bough
    Within the wood take heed.

" For they are spiteful brownies
    Who in the wood abide ;
So be thou careful of this thing,
    Lest evil should betide.

" But think not, little Mabel,
    Whilst thou art in the wood,
Of dwarfish, wilful brownies,
    But of the Father good.

" And when thou goest to the spring
    To fetch the water thence,
Do not disturb the little stream,
    Lest this should give offence.

" For the queen of all the fairies,
    She loves that water bright ;
I've seen her drinking there myself
    On many a summer night.

" But she's a gracious lady,
    And her thou needs't not fear ;
Only disturb thou not the stream,
    Nor spill the water clear."

" Now all this I will heed, mother,
  Will no word disobey,
And wait upon the grandmother
  This livelong summer day."

———

Part II.

Away tripped little Mabel,
  With the wheaten cake so fine,
With the new-made pat of butter,
  And the little flask of wine.

And long before the sun was hot,
  And the summer mist had cleared,
Beside the good old grandmother
  The willing child appeared.

And all her mother's message
  She told with right good-will,
How that the father was away,
  And the little child was ill.

And then she swept the hearth up clean,
  And then the table spread ;
And next she fed the dog and bird ;
  And then she made the bed.

" And go now," said the grandmother,
  " Ten paces down the dell,
And bring in water for the day, —
  Thou know'st the lady-well."

The first time that good Mabel went,
  Nothing at all saw she,
Except a bird, a sky-blue bird,
  That sat upon a tree.

The next time that good Mabel went,
  There sat a lady bright
Beside the well, — a lady small,
  All clothed in green and white.

A courtesy low made Mabel,
  And then she stooped to fill
Her pitcher at the sparkling spring,
  But no drop did she spill.

" Thou art a handy maiden,"
  The fairy lady said ;
" Thou hast not spilt a drop, nor yet
  The fairy spring troubled !

" And for this thing which thou hast done,
  Yet mayst not understand,
I give to thee a better gift
  Than houses or than land.

" Thou shalt do well whate'er thou dost,
  As thou hast done this day ;
Shalt have the will and power to please,
  And shalt be loved alway."

Thus having said, she passed from sight,
  And nought could Mabel see,
But the little bird, the sky-blue bird,
  Upon the leafy tree.

" And now go," said the grandmother,
  " And fetch in fagots dry ;
All in the neighboring fir-wood
  Beneath the trees they lie."

Away went kind, good Mabel,
  Into the fir-wood near,
Where all the ground was dry and brown,
  And the grass grew thin and sear.

She did not wander up and down,
  Nor yet a live branch pull,
But steadily of the fallen boughs
  She picked her apron full.

And when the wild-wood brownies
  Came sliding to her mind,
She drove them thence, as she was told,
  With home-thoughts sweet and kind.

But all that while the brownies
　　Within the fir-wood still,
They watched her how she picked the wood,
　　And strove to do no ill.

" And, oh, but she is small and neat,"
　　Said one ; " 'twere shame to spite
A creature so demure and meek,
　　A creature harmless quite ! "

" Look only," said another,
　　" At her little gown of blue :
At her kerchief pinned about her head,
　　And at her little shoe ! "

" Oh, but she is a comely child,"
　　Said a third ; " and we will lay
A good-luck penny in her path,
　　A boon for her this day, —
Seeing she broke no living wood ;
　　No live thing did affray ! "

With that the smallest penny,
　　Of the finest silver ore,
Upon the dry and slippery path,
　　Lay Mabel's feet before.

With joy she picked the penny up,
    The fairy penny good ;
And with her fagots dry and brown
    Went wandering from the wood.

" Now she has that," said the brownies,
    " Let flax be ever so dear,
'Twill buy her clothes of the very best,
    For many and many a year ! "

" And go now," said the grandmother,
    " Since falling is the dew,
Go down unto the lonesome glen,
    And milk the mother-ewe ! "

All down into the lonesome glen,
    Through copses thick and wild,
Through moist rank grass, by trickling streams,
    Went on the willing child.

And when she came to the lonesome glen,
    She kept beside the burn,
And neither plucked the strawberry-flower
    Nor broke the lady-fern.

And while she milked the mother-ewe
    Within this lonesome glen,
She wished that little Amy
    Were strong and well again.

And soon as she had thought this thought,
   She heard a coming sound,
As if a thousand fairy-folk
   Were gathering all around.

And then she heard a little voice,
   Shrill as the midge's wing,
That spake aloud, — " A human child
   Is here ; yet mark this thing, —

" The lady-fern is all unbroke,
   The strawberry-flower unta'en !
What shall be done for her who still
   From mischief can refrain ? "

" Give her a fairy cake ! " said one ;
   " Grant her a wish ! " said three :
" The latest wish that she hath wished,"
   Said all, " whate'er it be ! "

Kind Mabel heard the words they spake,
   And from the lonesome glen
Unto the good old grandmother
   Went gladly back again.

Thus happened it to Mabel
   On that midsummer day,
And these three fairy-blessings
   She took with her away.

'Tis good to make all duty sweet,
　　To be alert and kind ;
'Tis good, like little Mabel,
　　To have a willing mind.

MARY HOWITT.

———∘∘⦂⦁⦂∘∘———

I HEARD AN ANGEL.

———

I heard an angel singing,
When the day was springing :
" Mercy, pity, and peace
Are the world's release ! "

So he sang all day
Over the new-mown hay,
Till the sun went down,
And the hay-cocks looked brown.

BLAKE.

FAITH IN GOD.

I knew a widow very poor,
  Who four small children had:
The oldest was but six years old,
  A gentle, modest lad.

And very hard this widow toiled
  To feed her children four;
A noble heart the mother had,
  Though she was very poor.

To labor, she would leave her home,
  For children must be fed;
And glad was she when she could buy
  A shilling's worth of bread.

And this was all the children had
  On any day to eat:
They drank their water, ate their bread,
  But never tasted meat.

One day, when snow was falling fast,
  And piercing was the air,
I thought that I would go and see
  How these poor children were.

Ere long I reached their cheerless home —
  'Twas searched by every breeze —
When, going in, the eldest child
  I saw upon his knees.

I paused to listen to the boy :
  He never raised his head,
But still went on, and said, " Give us
  This day our daily bread."

I waited till the child was done,
  Still listening as he prayed ;
And when he rose, I asked him why
  That prayer he then had said.

" Why, sir," said he, " this morning, when
  My mother went away,
She wept, because she said she had
  No bread for us to-day.

" She said we children now must starve,
  Our father being dead ;
And then I told her not to cry,
  For I could get some bread.

" ' Our Father,' sir, the prayer begins,
  Which made me think that He,
As we have no kind father here,
  Would our kind Father be.

"And then you know, sir, that the prayer
   Asks God for bread each day ;
So in the corner, sir, I went,
   And that's what made me pray."

I quickly left that wretched room,
   And went with fleeting feet,
And very soon was back again
   With food enough to eat.

"I thought God heard me," said the boy ;
   I answered with a nod ;
I could not speak, but much I thought
   Of that boy's faith in God.

                       HAWKS.

NURSERY-SONG.

As I walked over the hill one day,
I listened, and heard a mother-sheep say,
" In all the green world there is nothing so sweet
As my little lammie, with his nimble feet ;
      With his eye so bright,
      And his wool so white,
Oh ! he is my darling, my heart's delight."
And the mother-sheep and her little one
Side by side lay down in the sun ;
And they went to sleep on the hill-side warm,
While my little lammie lies here on my arm.

I went to the kitchen, and what did I see
But the old gray cat with her kittens three !
I heard her whispering soft : said she,
" My kittens, with tails so cunningly curled,
Are the prettiest things that can be in the world.
      The bird on the tree,
      And the old ewe — she,
      May love their babies exceedingly ;
      But I love my kittens there,
      Under the rocking-chair.

I love my kittens with all my might,
I love them at morning, noon, and night.
Now I'll take up my kitties, the kitties I love,
And we'll lie down together beneath the warm stove."
Let the kittens sleep under the stove so warm,
While my little darling lies here on my arm.

I went to the yard, and I saw the old hen
Go clucking about with her chickens ten;
She clucked and she scratched and she bustled away,
And what do you think I heard the hen say?
I heard her say, " The sun never did shine
On anything like to these chickens of mine!
You may hunt the full moon and the stars, if you please,
But you never will find ten such chickens as these;
My dear downy darlings, my sweet little things,
Come, nestle now cosily under my wings."
                So the hen said,
                And the chickens all sped
As fast as they could to their nice feather-bed.
And there let them sleep in their feathers so warm,
While my little chick lies here on my arm.

MRS. CARTER.

THE ANGELS' WHISPER.

A baby was sleeping, its mother was weeping,
  For her husband was far on the wild, raging sea ;
And the tempest was swelling round the fisherman's
      dwelling,
    And she cried, " Dermot, darling, oh ! come back to
      me."

Her beads while she numbered, the baby still slumbered,
    And smiled in her face while she bended her knee.
" Oh ! blessed be that warning, my child, thy sleep
        adorning,
    For I know that the angels are whispering with thee.

" And while they are keeping bright watch o'er thy
        sleeping,
    Oh ! pray to them softly, my baby, with me ;
And say thou wouldst rather they'd watch o'er thy father,
    For I know that the angels are whispering with thee."

The dawn of the morning saw Dermot returning,
    And the wife wept with joy her babe's father to see ;
And closely caressing her child, with a blessing,
    Said, " I knew that the angels were whispering with
       thee."

LOVER.

I love it — I love it, and who shall dare
To chide me for loving that old arm-chair!
I've treasured it long as a sainted prize —
I've bedewed it with tears, I've embalmed it with sighs;

'Tis bound by a thousand bands to my heart,
Not a tie will break, not a link will start.
Would you learn the spell? — a mother sat there,
And a sacred thing is that old arm-chair.

In childhood's hour I lingered near
The hallowed seat with listening ear ;
And gentle words that mother would give,
To fit me to die, and teach me to live.
She told me shame would never betide,
With truth for my creed, and God for my Guide ;
She taught me to lisp my earliest prayer
As I knelt beside that old arm-chair.

I sat and watched her many a day,
When her eyes grew dim and her locks were gray,
And I almost worshipped her when she smiled
And turned from her Bible to bless her child.
Years rolled on, and the last one sped,
My idol was shattered — my earth-star fled :
I learnt how much the heart can bear
When I saw her die in that old arm-chair.

ELIZA COOK.

GRANDPAPA.

Grandpapa's hair is very white,
  And grandpapa walks but slow ;
He likes to sit still in his easy-chair,
  While the children come and go.
" Hush ! — play quietly," says mamma ;
" Let nobody trouble dear grandpapa."

Grandpapa's hand is thin and weak,
  It has worked hard all his days :
A strong right hand and an honest hand,
  That has won all good men's praise.
" Kiss it tenderly," says mamma ;
" Let every one honor grandpapa."

Grandpapa's eyes are growing dim ;
  They have looked on sorrow and death ;
But the love-light never went out of them,
  Nor the courage and the faith.
" You children, all of you," says mamma,
 " Have need to look up to dear grandpapa."

Grandpapa's years are wearing few,
    But he leaves a blessing behind —
A good life lived, and a good fight fought,
    True heart and equal mind.
  " Remember, my children," says mamma,
  " You bear the name of your grandpapa."

MRS. CRAIK.

FATHER WILLIAM.

" You are old, Father William," the young man cried ;
  " The few locks that are left you are gray ;
You are hale, Father William, a hearty old man ;
  Now tell me the reason, I pray."

" In the days of my youth," Father William replied,
  " I remembered that youth would fly fast ;
And abused not my health and my vigor at first,
  That I never might need them at last."

" You are old, Father William," the young man cried,
  " And pleasures with youth pass away ;
And yet you lament not the days that are gone ;
  Now tell me the reason, I pray."

"In the days of my youth," Father William replied,
  "I remembered that youth could not last;
I thought of the future, whatever I did,
  That I never might grieve for the past."

"You are old, Father William," the young man cried,
  "And life must be hast'ning away;
You are cheerful, and love to converse upon death;
  Now tell me the reason, I pray."

"I am cheerful, young man," Father William replied,
  "Let the cause thy attention engage:
In the days of my youth I remembered my God,
  And He hath not forgotten my age."

SOUTHEY.

A MASQUERADE.

A little old woman before me
  Went slowly down the street;
Walking as if aweary
  Were her feeble, tottering feet.

From under her old poke bonnet
  I caught a gleam of snow,
And her waving cap-string floated,
  Like a pennon, to and fro.

In the folds of her rusty mantle
  Sudden her footstep caught,
And I sprang to keep her from falling,
  With a touch as quick as thought.

When, under the old poke bonnet,
  I saw a winsome face,
Framed in with the flaxen ringlets
  Of my wee daughter Grace.

Mantle and cap together
  Dropped off at my very feet;
And there stood the little fairy,
  Beautiful, blushing, sweet!

Will it be like this, I wonder,
  When at last we come to stand
On the golden, ringing pavement
  Of the blesséd, blesséd land?

Losing the rusty garments
  We wore in the years of Time,
Will our better selves spring backward,
  Serene in a youth sublime?

Instead of the shapes that hid us,
   And made us old and gray,
Shall we get our child-hearts back again,
   With a brightness that will stay?

I thought — but my little daughter
   Slipped her dimpled hand in mine ;
" I was only playing," she whispered,
   " That I was ninety-nine."

———o○°○°○○———

THE GRAVES OF A HOUSEHOLD.

———

They grew in beauty, side by side,
   They filled one home with glee ;
Their graves are severed far and wide,
   By mount, and stream, and sea.

The same fond mother bent at night
   O'er each fair, sleeping brow ;
She had each folded flower in sight :
   Where are those sleepers now ?

One, midst the forest of the West,
   By a dark stream is laid ;
The Indian knows his place of rest,
   Far in the cedar shade.

THE GRAVES OF A HOUSEHOLD

The sea, the blue, lone sea, hath one ;
  He lies where pearls lie deep ;
He was the loved of all, yet none
  O'er his low bed may weep.

One sleeps where southern vines are dressed
  Above the noble slain ;
He wrapped the colors round his breast
  On a blood-red field of Spain.

And one — o'er her the myrtle showers
  Its leaves by soft winds fanned ;
She faded midst Italian flowers —
  The last of that fair band.

And parted thus, they rest who played
  Beneath the same green tree ;
Whose voices mingled as they prayed
  Around one parent knee.

They that with smiles lit up the hall,
  And cheered with song the hearth ;
Alas for love ! if thou wert all,
  And nought beyond, O earth !

                              MRS. HEMANS.

GEORGE NIDIVER.

Men have done brave deeds,
　　And bards have sung them well :
I of good George Nidiver
　　Now the tale will tell.

In Californian mountains
　　A hunter bold was he :
Keen his eye and sure his aim
　　As any you should see.

A little Indian boy
　　Followed him everywhere,
Eager to share the hunter's joy,
　　The hunter's meal to share.

And when the bird or deer
　　Fell by the hunter's skill,
The boy was always near
　　To help with right good-will.

One day as through the cleft
　　Between two mountains steep,
Shut in both right and left,
　　Their weary way they keep,

They see two grizzly bears,
  With hunger fierce and fell,
Rush at them unawares
  Right down the narrow dell.

The boy turned round with screams,
  And ran with terror wild;
One of the pair of savage beasts
  Pursued the shrieking child.

The hunter raised his gun, —
  He knew one charge was all, —
And through the boy's pursuing foe
  He sent his only ball.

The other on George Nidiver
  Came on with dreadful pace;
The hunter stood unarmed,
  And met him face to face.

I say *unarmed* he stood:
  Against those frightful paws
The rifle butt, or club of wood,
  Could stand no more than straws.

George Nidiver stood still
  And looked him in the face;
The wild beast stopped amazed,
  Then came with slack'ning pace.

Still firm the hunter stood,
  Although his heart beat high ;
Again the creature stopped,
  And gazed with wond'ring eye.

The hunter met his gaze,
  Nor yet an inch gave way ;
The bear turned slowly round,
  And slowly moved away.

What thoughts were in his mind
  It would be hard to spell ;
What thoughts were in George Nidiver
  I rather guess than tell.

But sure that rifle's aim,
  Swift choice of gen'rous part,
Showed in its passing gleam
  The depths of a brave heart.

THE IDLE SHEPHERD-BOYS.

The valley rings with mirth and joy;
   Among the hills the echoes play
A never, never-ending song,
   To welcome in the May.
The magpie chatters with delight;
   The mountain raven's youngling brood
Have left the mother and the nest,
And they go rambling east and west
   In search of their own food;
Or through the glitt'ring vapors dart
In very wantonness of heart.

Beneath a rock, upon the grass,
   Two boys are sitting in the sun;
It seems they have no work to do,
   Or that their work is done.

On pipes of sycamore they play
 The fragments of a Christmas hymn ;
Or with that plant which in our dale
We call stag-horn, or fox's tail,
 Their rusty hats they trim ;
And thus, as happy as the day,
Those shepherds wear the time away.

Along the river's stony marge
 The sand-lark chants a joyous song ;
The thrush is busy in the wood,
 And carols loud and strong ;
A thousand lambs are on the rocks,
 All newly born ; — both earth and sky
Keep jubilee ; and more than all,
Those boys with their green coronal ;
 They never hear the cry,
That plaintive cry ! which up the hill
Comes from the depth of Dungeon-Ghyll.

Said Walter, leaping from the ground,
 " Down to the stump of yon old yew
We'll for our whistles run a race."
 —— Away the shepherds flew.
They leapt — they ran — and when they came
 Right opposite to Dungeon-Ghyll,
Seeing that he should lose the prize,
" Stop ! " to his comrade Walter cries.

James stopped with no good will ;
Said Walter then, " Your task is here,
'Twill keep you working half a year.

" Now cross where I shall cross — come on,
 And follow me where I shall lead."
The other took him at his word,
 But did not like the deed.
It was a spot which you may see
 If ever you to Langdale go :
Into a chasm a mighty block
Hath fallen, and made a bridge of rock ;
 The gulf is deep below ;
And in a basin black and small
Receives a mighty waterfall.

With staff in hand across the cleft
 The challenger began his march ;
And now, all eyes and feet, hath gained
 The middle of the arch.
When, list ! he hears a piteous moan —
 Again ! — his heart within him dies —
His pulse is stopped, his breath is lost,
He totters, pale as any ghost,
 And, looking down, he spies
A lamb that in the pool is pent
Within that black and frightful rent.

The lamb had slipped into the stream,
   And safe without a bruise or wound
The cataract had borne him down
   Into the gulf profound.
His dam had seen him when he fell ;
   She saw him down the torrent borne ;
And, while with all a mother's love
'She from the lofty rocks above
   Sent forth a cry forlorn,
The lamb, still swimming round and round,
Made answer to the plaintive sound.

When he had learnt what thing it was
   That sent this rueful cry, I ween
The boy recovered heart, and told
   The sight which he had seen.
Both gladly now deferred their task ;
   Nor was there wanting other aid, —
A poet, one who loves the brooks
Far better than the sages' books,
   By chance had thither strayed ;
And there the helpless lamb he found,
By those huge rocks encompassed round.

He drew it gently from the pool,
   And brought it forth into the light ;
The shepherds met him with his charge,
   An unexpected sight !

Into their arms the lamb they took :
  Said they, " He's neither maimed nor scarred."
Then up the steep ascent they hied,
And placed him at his mother's side ;
  And gently did the bard
Those idle shepherd-boys upbraid,
And bade them better mind their trade.

                                        WORDSWORTH.

ALLEN–A–DALE.

Allen-a-Dale has no fagot for burning,
Allen-a-Dale has no furrow for turning,
Allen-a-Dale has no fleece for the spinning,
Yet Allen-a-Dale has red gold for the winning.
Come, read me my riddle ! come, hearken my tale,
And tell me the craft of bold Allen-a-Dale.

The Baron of Ravensworth prances in pride,
And he views his domains upon Arkindale side,
The mere for his net, and the land for his game,
The chase for the wild, and the park for the tame ;
Yet the fish of the lake and the deer of the vale
Are less free to Lord Dacre than Allen-a-Dale.

Allen-a-Dale was ne'er belted a knight,
Though his spur be as sharp, and his blade be as bright;
Allen-a-Dale is no baron or lord,
Yet twenty tall yeomen will draw at his word;
And the best of our nobles his bonnets will vail,
Who at Rere-cross on Stanmore meets Allen-a-Dale.

Allen-a-Dale to his wooing is come;
The mother, she asked of his household and home:
"Though the castle of Richmond stand fair on the hill,
My hall," quoth bold Allen, "shows gallanter still;
'Tis the blue vault of heaven, with its crescent so pale,
And with all its bright spangles!" said Allen-a-Dale.

The father was steel, and the mother was stone;
They lifted the latch, and they bade him be gone;
But loud, on the morrow, their wail and their cry:
He had laughed on the lass with his bonny black eye,
And she fled to the forest to hear a love-tale,
And the youth it was told by was Allen-a-Dale.

SCOTT.

ROBIN HOOD'S DEATH AND BURIAL.

When Robin Hood and Little John
  Went o'er yon bank of broom,
Said Robin Hood to Little John,
  " We have shot for many a pound ;

" But I am not able to shoot one shot more, —
  My arrows will not flee ;
But I have a cousin lives down below,
  Please God, she will bleed me."

Now Robin is to fair Kirkley gone,
  As fast as he can win ;
But before he came there, as we do hear,
  He was taken very ill.

And when that he came to fair Kirkley Hall,
  He knocked all at the ring,
But none was so ready as his cousin herself
  For to let bold Robin in.

" Will you please to sit down, cousin Robin," she said,
  " And drink some beer with me ? " —
" No, I will neither eat nor drink
  Till I am blooded by thee."

" Well, I have a room, cousin Robin," she said,
  " Which you did never see,
And if you please to walk therein,
  You blooded by me shall be."

She took him by the lily-white hand,
  And led him to a private room,
And there she blooded bold Robin Hood
  Whilst one drop of blood would run.

She blooded him in the vein of the arm,
  And locked him up in the room ;
There did he bleed all the livelong day,
  Until the next day at noon.

He then bethought him of a casement door,
  Thinking for to be gone :
He was so weak he could not leap,
  And he could not get down.

He then bethought him of his bugle-horn,
  Which hung low down to his knee ;
He set his horn unto his mouth,
  And blew out weak blasts three.

Then Little John, when hearing him,
  As he sat under the tree,
" I fear my master is near dead,
  He blows so wearilee."

Then Little John to fair Kirkley is gone,
  As fast as he can flee;
But when he came to Kirkley Hall,
  He broke locks two or three;

Until he came bold Robin to,
  Then he fell on his knee:
"A boon, a boon," cries Little John,
  "Master, I beg of thee."

"What is that boon," quoth Robin Hood,
  "Little John, thou begs of me?" —
"It is, to burn fair Kirkley Hall,
  And all their nunnerie."

" Now nay, now nay," quoth Robin Hood,
   " That boon I'll not grant thee ;
I never hurt woman in all my life,
   Nor man in woman's companie.

" I never hurt fair maid in all my time,
   Nor at my end shall it be.
But give me my bent bow in my hand,
   And a broad arrow I'll let flee,

" And where this arrow is taken up,
   There shall my grave digged be.
Lay me a green sod under my head,
   And another at my feet,

" And lay my bent bow by my side,
   Which was my music sweet ;
And make my grave of gravel and green,
   Which is most right and meet.

" Let me have length and breadth enough,
   With a green sod under my head,
That they may say, when I am dead,
   Here lies bold Robin Hood."

These words they readily promised him,
   Which did bold Robin please ;
And there they buried bold Robin Hood,
   Near to the fair Kirkléys.

OLD BALLAD.

WHAT THE WINDS BRING.

———

" Which is the wind that brings the cold ? " —
  " The North-wind, Freddy — and all the snow ;
And the sheep will scamper into the fold,
  When the North begins to blow."

" Which is the wind that brings the heat ? " —
  " The South-wind, Katy ; and corn will grow,
And peaches redden, for you to eat,
  When the South begins to blow."

" Which is the wind that brings the rain ? " —
  " The East-wind, Arty ; and farmers know
That cows come shivering up the lane,
  When the East begins to blow."

" Which is the wind that brings the flowers ? " —
  " The West-wind, Bessy ; and soft and low
The birdies sing in the summer hours,
  When the West begins to blow."

STEDMAN.

IN MARCH.

The cock is crowing,
The stream is flowing,
The small birds twitter,
The lake doth glitter,
The green field sleeps in the sun ;
The oldest and youngest
Are at work with the strongest ;
The cattle are grazing,
Their heads never raising ;
There are forty feeding like one !

Like an army defeated,
The snow hath retreated,
And now doth fare ill
On the top of the bare hill ;
The ploughboy is whooping — anon — anon.
There's joy in the mountains ;
There's life in the fountains ;
Small clouds are sailing,
Blue sky prevailing ;
The rain is over and gone !

WORDSWORTH.

MARCH.

The stormy March is come at last,
   With wind, and cloud, and changing skies;
I hear the rushing of the blast
   That through the snowy valley flies.

Ah, passing few are they who speak,
   Wild, stormy month! in praise of thee;
Yet, though thy winds are loud and bleak,
   Thou art a welcome month to me.

For thou, to northern lands, again
   The glad and glorious sun dost bring,
And thou hast joined the gentle train,
   And wear'st the gentle name of Spring.

And, in thy reign of blast and storm,
   Smiles many a long, bright, sunny day,
When the changed winds are soft and warm,
   And heaven puts on the blue of May.

Thou bring'st the hope of those calm skies,
   And that soft time of sunny showers,
When the wide bloom, on earth that lies,
   Seems of a brighter world than ours.

                              BRYANT.

CHILD TO A ROSE.

"WHITE Rose, talk to me;
    I don't know what to do.
    Why do you say no word to me,
      Who say so much to you?
I'm bringing you a little rain;
    And I shall be so proud,
If, when you feel it on your face,
    You take me for a cloud.
Here I come so softly,
    You cannot hear me walking:
If I take you by surprise,
    I may catch you talking.

White Rose, are you tired
    Of staying in one place?
Do you ever wish to see
    The wild flowers face to face?
Do you know the woodbines,
    And the big brown crested reeds?
Do you wonder how they live
    So friendly with the weeds?

Have you any work to do
  When you've finished growing?
Shall you teach your little buds
  Pretty ways of blowing?

Do you ever go to sleep?
  Once I woke by night
And looked out of the window,
  And there you stood moon-white, —
Moon-white in a mist of darkness, —
  With never a word to say;
But you seemed to move a little,
  And then I ran away.
I should have felt no wonder
  After I hid my head,
If I had found you standing
  Moon-white beside my bed.

White Rose, do you love me?
  I only wish you'd say.
I would work hard to please you,
  If I but knew the way.
It seems so hard to be loving,
  And not a sign to see
But the silence and the sweetness
  For all as well as me.

I think you nearly perfect,
  In spite of all your scorns;
But, White Rose, if I were you,
  I wouldn't have those thorns.

POEMS FOR A CHILD.

———◦○┇◦◦———

THE MOUNTAIN AND THE SQUIRREL.

The mountain and the squirrel
Had a quarrel,
And the former called the latter " Little prig ! "
Bun replied,
" You are doubtless very big,
But all sorts of things and weather
Must be taken in together
To make up a year,
And a sphere :
And I think it no disgrace
To occupy my place.
If I'm not so large as you,
You are not so small as I,
And not half so spry ;
I'll not deny you make
A very pretty squirrel track.
Talents differ; all is well and wisely put ;
If I cannot carry forests on my back,
Neither can you crack a nut."   R. W. EMERSON.

THE WARY TROUT.

Down in the deep
Dark holes I keep,
And there in the noontide I float and sleep :
By the hemlock log,
And the springing bog,
And the arching alders I lie incog.

The angler's fly
Comes dancing by,
But never a moment it cheats my eye ;
For the wary trout
Is not such a lout
As to be by a wading boy pulled out.

King of the brook,
No fisher's hook
Fills me with dread of the toiling cook ;
But here I lie
And laugh as they try ;
Shall I bite at their bait?   No, no ; not I.

But when the streams,
With moonlight beams,

Sparkle all silver and starlight gleams,
Then, then look out
For the wary trout;
For he springs and dimples the shallows about,
While the tired angler dreams.

————o o̶:̶o̶:̶o o————

BOYS' PLAY AND GIRLS' PLAY.

———

" Now, let's have a game of play,
Lucy, Jane, and little May.
I will be a grizzly bear,
Prowling here and prowling there,
Sniffing round and round about,
Till I find you children out;
And my dreadful den shall be
Deep within the hollow tree."

" Oh, no ! please not, Robert, dear,
Do not be a grizzly bear :
Little May was half afraid
When she heard the noise you made,
Roaring like a lion strong,
Just now as you came along ;
And she'll scream and start to-night,
If you give her any fright."

"Well, then, I will be a fox!
You shall be the hens and cocks,
In the farmer's apple-tree,
Crowing out so lustily.
I will softly creep this way —
Peep — and pounce upon my prey;
And I'll bear you to my den —
Where the fern grows in the glen."

"Oh, no, Robert! you're so strong,
While you're dragging us along
I'm afraid you'll tear our frocks.
We won't play at hens and cocks." —
"If you won't play fox or bears,
I'm a dog, and you be hares;
Then you'll only have to run.
Girls are never up to fun."

"You've your play, and we have ours,
   Go and climb the trees again.
   I, and little May, and Jane,
Are so happy with our flowers.
   Jane is culling foxglove bells,
May and I are making posies,
   And we want to search the dells
For the latest summer roses."

MRS. HAWTREY.

JOHN GILPIN.

John Gilpin was a citizen
   Of credit and renown,
A train-band captain eke was he
   Of famous London town.

John Gilpin's spouse said to her dear,
   " Though wedded we have been
These twice ten tedious years, yet we
   No holiday have seen.

" To-morrow is our wedding-day,
   And we will then repair
Unto the ' Bell ' at Edmonton,
   All in a chaise and pair.

" My sister, and my sister's child,
   Myself and children three,
Will fill the chaise ; so you must ride
   On horseback after we."

He soon replied, " I do admire
   Of womankind but one ;
And you are she, my dearest dear,
   Therefore it shall be done.

" I am a linen-draper bold
    As all the world doth know,
        And my good friend the calender
            Will lend his horse to go."

            Quoth Mrs. Gilpin, " That's
                well said ;
                And for that wine is dear,
        We will be furnished with
                our own,
                Which is both bright and
                    clear."

John Gilpin kissed his loving wife,
    O'erjoyed was he to find
That, though on pleasure she was bent,
    She had a frugal mind.

The morning came, the chaise was brought,
But yet was not allowed
To drive up to the door, lest all
Should say that she was proud.

So three doors off the chaise was stayed,
Where they did all get in, —
Six precious souls, and all agog
To dash through thick and thin.

Smack went the whip, round went the wheels,
Were never folks so glad!
The stones did rattle underneath
As if Cheapside were mad.

John Gilpin at his horse's side
Seized fast the flowing mane,
And up he got, in haste to ride,
But soon came down again: —

For saddle-tree scarce reached had he,
His journey to begin,
When, turning round his head, he saw
Three customers come in.

So down he came; for loss of time,
Although it grieved him sore,
Yet loss of pence, full well he knew,
Would trouble him much more.

'Twas long before the customers
  Were suited to their mind,
When Betty, screaming, came downstairs,
  " The wine is left behind ! "

" Good lack ! " quoth he ; " yet bring it me,
  My leathern belt likewise,
In which I bear my trusty sword
  When I do exercise."

Now, Mistress Gilpin (careful soul !)
  Had two stone bottles found,
To hold the liquor that she loved,
  And keep it safe and sound.

Each bottle had a curling ear,
  Through which the belt he drew,
And hung a bottle on each side,
  To make his balance true.

Then over all, that he might be
  Equipped from top to toe,
His long red cloak, well brushed and neat,
  He manfully did throw.

Now see him mounted once again
  Upon his nimble steed,
Full slowly pacing o'er the stones
  With caution and good heed.

But finding soon a smoother road
   Beneath his well-shod feet,
The snorting beast began to trot,
   Which galled him in his seat.

" So ! fair and softly, John," he cried ;
   But John he cried in vain :
That trot became a gallop soon,
   In spite of curb and rein.

So, stooping down, as needs he must
   Who cannot sit upright,
He grasped the mane with both his hands,
   And eke with all his might.

His horse, which never in that sort
   Had handled been before,
What thing upon his back had got
   Did wonder more and more.

Away went Gilpin, neck or nought,
   Away went hat and wig :
He little dreamt, when he set out,
   Of running such a rig.

The wind did blow, the cloak did fly
   Like streamer long and gay,
Till loop and button, failing both,
   At last it flew away.

Then might all people well discern
　　The bottles he had slung, —
A bottle swinging at each side,
　　As hath been said or sung.

The dogs did bark, the children screamed,
　　Up flew the windows all,
And every soul cried out, " Well done ! "
　　As loud as he could bawl.

Away went Gilpin — who but he?
　　His fame soon spread around :
" He carries weight ! he rides a race !
　　'Tis for a thousand pound ! "

And still, as fast as he drew near,
　　'Twas wonderful to view,
How in a trice the turnpike-men
　　Their gates wide open threw.

And now, as he went bowing down
　　His reeking head full low,
The bottles twain behind his back
　　Were shattered at a blow.

Down ran the wine into the road,
　　Most piteous to be seen,
Which made his horse's flanks to smoke
　　As they had basted been.

But still he seemed to carry weight,
   With leathern girdle braced ;
For all might see the bottle-necks
   Still dangling at his waist.

Thus all through merry Islington
   These gambols he did play,
Until he came unto the Wash
   Of Edmonton so gay ;

And there he threw the Wash about
   On both sides of the way,
Just like unto a trundling mop,
   Or a wild goose at play.

At Edmonton his loving wife
   From the balcony espied
Her tender husband, wond'ring much
   To see how he did ride.

" Stop, stop, John Gilpin ! Here's the house,"
   They all aloud did cry ;
" The dinner waits, and we are tired." —
   Said Gilpin, " So am I."

But yet his horse was not a whit
   Inclined to tarry there ;
For why? — his owner had a house
   Full ten miles off, at Ware.

So like an arrow swift he flew,
  Shot by an archer strong;
So did he fly — which brings me to
  The middle of my song.

Away went Gilpin, out of breath,
  And sore against his will,
Till at his friend the calender's
  His horse at last stood still.

The calender, amazed to see
  His neighbor in such trim,
Laid down his pipe, flew to the gate,
  And thus accosted him:

" What news? what news? your tidings tell;
  Tell me you must and shall;
Say why bareheaded you are come,
  Or why you come at all?"

Now, Gilpin had a pleasant wit,
  And loved a timely joke,
And thus unto the calender
  In merry guise he spoke:

" I came because your horse would come;
  And, if I well forebode,
My hat and wig will soon be here —
  They are upon the road."

The calender, right glad to find
   His friend in merry pin,
Returned him not a single word,
   But to the house went in;

Whence straight he came with hat and wig, —
   A wig that flowed behind,
A hat not much the worse for wear, —
   Each comely in its kind.

He held them up, and in his turn
   Thus showed his ready wit:
" My head is twice as big as yours,
   They therefore needs must fit.

" But let me scrape the dirt away
   That hangs upon your face;
And stop and eat, for well you may
   Be in a hungry case."

Said John, " It is my wedding-day,
   And all the world would stare
If wife should dine at Edmonton,
   And I should dine at Ware."

So, turning to his horse, he said,
   " I am in haste to dine;
'Twas for *your* pleasure you came here,
   You shall go back for *mine*."

Ah, luckless speech and bootless boast!
  For which he paid full dear ;
For while he spake a braying ass
  Did sing most loud and clear ;

Whereat his horse did snort, as he
  Had heard a lion roar,
And galloped off with all his might,
  As he had done before.

Away went Gilpin, and away
　Went Gilpin's hat and wig ;
He lost them sooner than at first ;
　For why ? — they were too big.

Now, Mistress Gilpin, when she saw
　Her husband posting down
Into the country far away,
　She pulled out half-a-crown ;

And thus unto the youth she said
　That drove them to the " Bell,"
" This shall be yours when you bring back
　My husband safe and well."

The youth did ride, and soon did meet
　John coming back amain ;
Whom in a trice he tried to stop
　By catching at his rein ;

But not performing what he meant,
　And gladly would have done,
The frighted steed he frighted more,
　And made him faster run.

Away went Gilpin, and away
　Went postboy at his heels ;
The postboy's horse right glad to miss
　The lumbering of the wheels.

Six gentlemen upon the road,
  Thus seeing Gilpin fly
With postboy scamp'ring in the rear,
  They raised the hue and cry:

" Stop thief! stop thief! a highwayman!"
  Not one of them was mute;
And all and each that passed that way
  Did join in the pursuit.

And now the turnpike-gates again
  Flew open in short space,
The tollmen thinking as before
  That Gilpin rode a race.

And so he did; and won it too,
  For he got first to town;
Nor stopped till where he had got up
  He did again get down.

Now let us sing, Long live the king,
  And Gilpin, long live he;
And when he next doth ride abroad,
  May I be there to see!

COWPER.

CONTENTED JOHN.

One honest John Tomkins, a hedger and ditcher,
Although he was poor, did not want to be richer ;
For all such vain wishes in him were prevented
By a fortunate habit of being contented.

Though cold was the weather, or dear was the food,
John never was found in a murmuring mood ;
For this he was constantly heard to declare, —
What he could not prevent he would cheerfully bear.

"For why should I grumble and murmur?" he said ;
"If I cannot get meat, I can surely get bread ;
And, though fretting may make my calamities deeper,
It can never cause bread and cheese to be cheaper."

If John was afflicted with sickness or pain,
He wished himself better, but did not complain,
Nor lie down and fret in despondence and sorrow,
But said that he hoped to be better to-morrow.

If any one wronged him or treated him ill,
Why, John was good-natured and sociable still ;
For he said that revenging the injury done
Would be making two rogues when there need be but one.

And thus honest John, though his station was humble,
Passed through this sad world without even a grumble ;
And I wish that some folks, who are greater and richer,
Would copy John Tomkins, the hedger and ditcher.

JANE TAYLOR.

I WOULD I WERE A NOTE.

I would I were a note
From a sweet bird's throat !
I'd float on forever,
And melt away never.
I would I were a note
From a sweet bird's throat !

But I am what I am !
As content as a lamb,
No new state I'll covet ;
For how long should I love it ?
No, I'll be what I am, —
As content as a lamb !

WISHING.

Ring–ting! I wish I were a Primrose,
A bright yellow Primrose, blowing in the spring!
 The stooping boughs above me,
 The wand'ring bee to love me,
The fern and moss to creep across,
 And the Elm-tree for our king!

Nay — stay! I wish I were an Elm-tree,
A great, lofty Elm-tree, with green leaves gay!
 The winds would set them dancing,
 The sun and moonshine glance in,
The birds would house among the boughs,
 And sweetly sing.

Oh — no! I wish I were a Robin,
A Robin or a little Wren, everywhere to go;
 Through forest, field, or garden,
 And ask no leave or pardon,
Till winter comes with icy thumbs
 To ruffle up our wing!

Well — tell!   Where should I fly to,
Where go to sleep in the dark wood or dell?
    Before a day was over,
    Home comes the rover,
For mother's kiss — sweeter this
    Than any other thing.

ALLINGHAM.

GIVE ME A WISH.

———

" Be my fairy, mother,
  Give me a wish a day ;
Something, as well in sunshine
  As when the rain-drops play."

" And if I were a fairy,
  With but one wish to spare,
What should I give thee, darling,
  To quiet thine earnest prayer?"

" I'd like a little brook, mother,
  All for my very own, —
To laugh all day among the trees,
  And shine on the mossy stone ;

" To run right under the window,
  And sing me fast asleep ;
With soft steps and a tender sound,
  Over the grass to creep.

" Make it run down the hill, mother,
  With a leap like a tinkling bell,
So fast I never can catch the leaf
  That into its fountain fell.

"Make it as wild as a frightened bird,
   As crazy as a bee,
With a noise like the baby's funny laugh ; —
   That's the brook for me!"

ROSE TERRY.

———∘∘∘∘∘———

UNDER THE GREENWOOD TREE.

Under the greenwood tree,
Who loves to lie with me,
And tune his merry note
Unto the sweet bird's throat.
Come hither, come hither, come hither!
   Here shall he see
      No enemy,
But winter and rough weather.

Who doth ambition shun,
And loves to lie i' the sun,
Seeking the food he eats,
And pleased with what he gets,
Come hither, come hither, come hither!
   Here shall he see
      No enemy,
But winter and rough weather.

SHAKESPEARE.

WE ARE SEVEN.

. . . . . . A simple child
  That lightly draws its breath,
And feels its life in every limb,
  What should it know of death?

I met a little cottage-girl :
  She was eight years old, she said ;
Her hair was thick with many a curl
  That clustered round her head.

She had a rustic, woodland air,
  And she was wildly clad ;
Her eyes were bright, and very fair —
  Her beauty made me glad.

" Sisters and brothers, little maid,
  How many may you be ? " —
" How many?   Seven in all," she said,
  And wond'ring looked at me.

" And where are they?   I pray you tell."
  She answered, " Seven are we ;
And two of us at Conway dwell,
  And two are gone to sea.

" Two of us in the church-yard lie,
  My sister and my brother ;
And, in the church-yard cottage, I
  Dwell near them with my mother."

" You say that two at Conway dwell,
  And two are gone to sea,
Yet ye are seven? — I pray you tell,
  Sweet maid, how this may be ? "

Then did the little maid reply,
  " Seven boys and girls are we ;
Two of us in the church-yard lie,
  Beneath the church-yard tree."

" You run about, my little maid,
  Your limbs they are alive :
If two are in the church-yard laid,
  Then ye are only five."

" Their graves are green, they may be seen,"
  The little maid replied,
" Twelve steps or more from my mother's door,
  And they are side by side.

" My stockings there I often knit,
  My kerchief there I hem ;
And there upon the ground I sit —
  I sit and sing to them.

" And often after sunset, sir,
  When it is light and fair,
I take my little porringer,
  And eat my supper there.

" The first that died was little Jane ;
  In bed she moaning lay,
Till God released her of her pain,
  And then she went away.

" So in the church-yard she was laid ;
  And when the grass was dry
Together round her grave we played,
  My brother John and I.

" And when the ground was white with snow,
  And I could run and slide,
My brother John was forced to go,
  And he lies by her side."

" How many are you, then," said I,
  " If they two are in heaven ? "
The little maiden did reply,
  " O master ! we are seven."

" But they are dead ; these two are dead !
  Their spirits are in heaven ! "
'Twas throwing words away ; for still
The little maid would have her will,
  And said, " Nay, we are seven ! "

WORDSWORTH.

THE STRANGE CHILD'S CHRISTMAS.

There went a stranger child,
　　As Christmas Eve closed in,
Through the streets of a town, whose windows shone
　　With the warmth and light within.

It stopped at every house,
　　The Christmas-tree to see
On that festive night, when they shone so bright —
　　And it sighed right bitterly.

Then wept the child, and said,
　　" This night hath every one
A Christmas-tree, that he glad may be,
　　And I alone have none.

" Ah ! when I lived at home,
　　From brother's and sister's hand
I had my share, but there's none to care
　　For me in the stranger's land.

" Will no one let me in?
　　No presents I would crave,
But to see the light, and the tree all bright,
　　And the gifts that others have."

At shutter, and door, and gate
    It knocks with a timid hand ;
But none will mark where alone in the dark
    That little child doth stand.

Each father brings home gifts,
    Each mother, kind and mild ;
There is joy for all, but none will call
    And welcome that lonely child.

" Mother and father are dead —
O Jesus, kind and dear,
I've no one now, there is none but Thou,
For I am forgotten here ! "

The poor child rubs its hands,
All frozen and numbed with cold,
And draws round its head, with shrinking dread,
Its garment worn and old.

But see — another Child
Comes gliding through the street,
And its robe is white, in its hand a light ;
It speaks, and its voice is sweet :

" Once on this earth a Child
I lived, as thou livest yet ;
Though all turn away from thee to-day,
Yet I will not forget.

" Each child, with equal love,
I hold beneath my care, —
In the street's dull gloom, in the lighted room,
I am with them everywhere.

" Here, in the darkness dim,
I'll show thee, child, thy tree ;
Those that spread their light through the chambers bright
So lovely scarce can be."

And with its white hand points
The Christ-child to the sky,
And, lo ! afar, with each lamp a star,
A tree gleamed there on high.

So far, and yet so near,
The light shone overhead ;
And all was well, for the child could tell
For whom that tree was spread.

It gazed as in a dream,
And angels bent and smiled,
And with outstretched hand to that brighter land
They carried the stranger child.

And the little one went home
With its Saviour Christ to stay,
All the hunger and cold and the pain of old
Forgotten and past away.

FROM THE GERMAN.

A STORY BY THE FIRE.

Children love to hear of children!
    I will tell of a little child
Who dwelt alone with his mother
    By the edge of a forest wild.
One summer eve from the forest,
    Late, late, down the grassy track,
The child came back with lingering step,
    And looks oft turning back.

" O mother ! " he said, " in the forest
    I have met with a little child ;
All day he played with me — all day
    He talked with me and smiled.
At last he left me alone, but then
    He gave me this rosebud red ;
And said he would come to me again
    When all its leaves were spread.

" I will put my rosebud in a glass,
    I will watch it night and day.
Dear little friend, wilt thou come again?
    Wilt thou come by my side to play?

I will seek for strawberries — the best
  Of all shall be for thee ;
I will show thee the eggs in the linnet's nest
  None know about but me."

At morn, beside the window-sill,
  Awoke a bird's clear song ;
But all within the house was still, —
  The child was sleeping long.
The mother went to his little room, —
  With all its leaves outspread
She saw a rose in fullest bloom ;
  And, in the little bed,
A child that did not breathe nor stir, —
  A little happy child, —
Who had met his little friend again,
  And in the meeting smiled.

DORA GREENWELL.

CASABIANCA.

The boy stood on the burning deck,
  Whence all but him had fled;
The flame that lit the battle's wreck
  Shone round him o'er the dead;

Yet beautiful and bright he stood,
　　As born to rule the storm ;
A creature of heroic blood,
　　A proud, though childlike form.

The flames rolled on — he would not go
　　Without his father's word ;
That father, faint in death below,
　　His voice no longer heard.

He called aloud, " Say, father ! say,
　　If yet my task is done."
He knew not that the chieftain lay
　　Unconscious of his son.

" Speak, father ! " once again he cried,
　　" If I may yet be gone ; "
And but the booming shots replied,
　　And fast the flames rolled on.

Upon his brow he felt their breath,
　　And in his waving hair,
And looked from that lone post of death,
　　In still, but brave despair ;

And shouted but once more aloud,
　　" My father ! must I stay ? "
While o'er him fast, through sail and shroud,
　　The wreathing fires made way.

They wrapt the ship in splendor wild,
  They caught the flag on high,
And streamed above the gallant child
  Like banners in the sky.

There came a burst of thunder sound —
  The boy — oh ! where was he ?
Ask of the winds, that far around
  With fragments strewed the sea,

With mast, and helm, and pennon fair,
  That well had borne their part ;
But the noblest thing that perished there
  Was that young faithful heart !

Mrs. Hemans.

TOM BOWLING.

Here, a sheer hulk, lies poor Tom Bowling,
  The darling of our crew ;
No more he'll hear the tempest howling,
  For Death has broached him to ;
His form was of the manliest beauty,
  His heart was kind and soft ;
Faithful below he did his duty,
  But now he's gone aloft.

Tom never from his word departed,
   His virtues were so rare ;
His friends were many and true-hearted,
   His Poll was kind and fair ;
And then he'd sing so blithe and jolly,
   Ah, many's the time and oft!
But mirth is turned to melancholy,
   For Tom is gone aloft.

Yet shall poor Tom find pleasant weather,
   When He, who all commands,
Shall give, to call life's crew together,
   The word to pipe all hands.
Thus Death, who kings and tars despatches,
   In vain Tom's life has doffed ;
For though his body's under hatches,
   His soul is gone aloft.

DIBDIN.

BLACK-EYED SUSAN.

All in the Downs the fleet was moored,
   The streamers waving in the wind,
When Black-eyed Susan came on board,
   " Oh, where shall I my true-love find ?
Tell me, ye jovial sailors, tell me true,
Does my sweet William sail among your crew ? "

William, who high upon the yard,
　　Rocked by the billows to and fro,
Soon as the well-known voice he heard,
　　He sighed and cast his eyes below ;
The cord flies swiftly through his glowing hands,
And quick as lightning on the deck he stands.

" O Susan, Susan, lovely dear,
　　My vows shall always true remain ;
Let me kiss off that falling tear, —
　　We only part to meet again ;
Change as ye list, ye winds, my heart shall be
The faithful compass that still points to thee.

" Believe not what the landsmen say,
　　Who tempt with doubts thy constant mind ;
They tell thee sailors, when away,
　　In every port a mistress find ; —
Yes, yes, believe them when they tell you so,
For thou art present wheresoe'er I go."

The boatswain gave the dreadful word,
　　The sails their swelling bosoms spread ;
No longer she must stay on board, —
　　They kissed, she sighed — he hung his head.
Her lessening boat unwilling rows to land,
" Adieu ! " she cried, and waved her lily hand.

GAY.

THE SANDS OF DEE.

"O, Mary, go and call the cattle home,
 And call the cattle home,
And call the cattle home,
 Across the sands o' Dee."
The western wind was wild and dank wi' foam,
 And all alone went she.

The creeping tide came up along the sand,
 And o'er and o'er the sand,
And round and round the sand,
 As far as eye could see ;
The blinding mist came down and hid the land —
 And never home came she.

Oh, is it weed, or fish, or floating hair —
 And tress o' golden hair,
O' drownéd maiden's hair,
 Above the nets at sea?
Was never salmon yet that shone so fair,
 Among the stakes o' Dee."

They rowed her in across the rolling foam,
  The cruel, crawling foam,
The cruel, hungry foam,
  To her grave beside the sea:
But still the boatmen hear her call the cattle home,
  Across the sands o' Dee.

KINGSLEY.

A WET SHEET AND A FLOWING SEA.

A wet sheet and a flowing sea,
  A wind that follows fast,
And fills the white and rustling sail,
  And bends the gallant mast;
And bends the gallant mast, my boys!
  While, like the eagle free,
Away the good ship flies, and leaves
  Old England on the lee.

"Oh, for a soft and gentle wind!"
  I heard a fair one cry;
But oh, give me the swelling breeze,
  And white waves heaving high;

And white waves heaving high, my boys,
  The good ship tight and free!
The world of waters is our home,
  And merry men are we.

There's tempest in yon hornéd moon,
  And lightning in yon cloud;
And hark the music, mariners!
  The wind is piping loud;
The wind is piping loud, my boys!
  The lightning flashing free,
While the hollow oak our palace is,
  Our heritage the sea.

CUNNINGHAM.

THE BAY OF BISCAY.

Loud roared the dreadful thunder,
  The rain a deluge showers,
The clouds were rent asunder
  By lightning's vivid powers;
The night both drear and dark,
  Our poor devoted bark
There she lay till next day,
  In the Bay of Biscay, O!

Now dashed upon the billow,
  Our opening timbers creak;
Each fears a watery pillow, —
  None stops the dreadful leak;
To cling to slippery shrouds
  Each breathless seaman crowds,
As she lay, till the day,
  In the Bay of Biscay, O!

At length the wished-for morrow
  Broke through the hazy sky;
Absorbed in silent sorrow,
  Each heaved a bitter sigh;
The dismal wreck to view
  Struck horror to the crew,
As she lay, on that day,
  In the Bay of Biscay, O!

Her yielding timbers sever,
  Her pitchy seams are rent,
When Heaven, all bounteous ever,
  Its boundless mercy sent;
A sail in sight appears,
  We hail her with three cheers:
Now we sail, with the gale,
  From the Bay of Biscay, O!

CHERRY.

THE WIVES OF BRIXHAM.

A TRUE STORY.

The merry boats of Brixham
  Go out to search the seas ;
A staunch and sturdy fleet are they,
  Who love a swinging breeze ;
And before the woods of Devon,
  And the silver cliffs of Wales,
You may see, when summer evenings fall,
  The light upon their sails.

But when the year grows darker,
  And gray winds hunt the foam,
They go back to Little Brixham,
  And ply their toil at home.
And thus it chanced one winter's night,
  When a storm began to roar,
That all the men were out at sea,
  And all the wives on shore.

Then as the wind grew fiercer,
  The women's cheeks grew white, —
It was fiercer in the twilight,
  And fiercest in the night.
The strong clouds set themselves like ice,
  Without a star to melt;
The blackness of the darkness
  Was darkness to be felt.

The old men they were anxious,
  They dreaded what they knew;
What do you think the women did?
  Love taught them what to do!
Outspake a wife, " We've beds at home,
  We'll burn them for a light, —
Give us the men, and the bare ground,
  We want no more to-night."

They took the grandame's blanket,
  Who shivered and bade them go
They took the baby's pillow,
  Who could not say them no;
And they heaped a great fire on the pier,
  And knew not all the while
If they were heaping a bonfire,
  Or only a funeral pile.

And fed with precious food, the flame
    Shone bravely on the black,
Till a cry rang through the people.
    "A boat is coming back!"
Staggering dimly through the fog
    Come shapes of fear and doubt,
But when the first prow strikes the pier,
    Cannot you hear them shout?

Then all along the breath of flame,
  Dark figures shrieked and ran,
With, " Child, here comes your father ! "
  Or, " Wife, is this your man ? "
And faint feet touch the welcome shore,
  And wait a little while ;
And kisses drop from frozen lips,
  Too tired to speak or smile.

So, one by one, they struggled in
  All that the sea would spare ;
We will not reckon through our tears
  The names that were not there ;
But some went home without a bed,
  When all the tale was told,
Who were too cold with sorrow
  To know the night was cold.

And this is what the men must do
  Who work in wind and foam ;
And this is what the women bear
  Who watch for them at home.
So when you see a Brixham boat
  Go out to face the gales,
Think of the love that travels
  Like light upon her sails !

POEMS FOR A CHILD.

THE NORTHERN SEAS.

Up! up! let us a voyage take;
  Why sit we here at ease?
Find us a vessel tight and snug,
    Bound for the Northern Seas.

I long to see the northern lights
    With their rushing splendors fly,
Like living things with flaming wings,
    Wide o'er the wondrous sky.

I long to see those icebergs vast,
    With heads all crowned with snow,
Whose green roots sleep in the awful deep,
    Two hundred fathoms low.

I long to hear the thundering crash
    Of their terrific fall,
And the echoes from a thousand cliffs
    Like lonely voices call.

There shall we see the fierce white bear,
    The sleepy seals aground,
And the spouting whales that to and fro
    Sail with a dreary sound.

There may we tread on depths of ice,
   That the hairy mammoth hide ;
Perfect as when, in times of old,
   The mighty creature died.

And while the unsetting sun shines on
   Through the still heaven's deep blue,
We'll traverse the azure waves, the herds
   Of the dread sea-horse to view.

We'll pass the shores of solemn pine,
 Where wolves and black bears prowl ;
And away to the rocky isles of mist,
 To rouse the northern fowl.

Up there shall start ten thousand wings
 With a rustling, whistling din ;
Up shall the auk and fulmar start,
 All but the fat penguin.

And there in the wastes of the silent sky,
 With the silent earth below,
We shall see far off to his lonely rock
 The lonely eagle go.

Then softly, softly will we tread
 By inland streams, to see
Where the pelican of the silent North
 Sits there all silently.

MARY HOWITT.

WINSTANLEY.

Winstanley's deed, you kindly folk,
   With it I fill my lay,
And a nobler man ne'er walked the world,
   Let his name be what it may.

The good ship Snowdrop tarried long;
   Up at the vane looked he;
"Belike," he said, for the wind had dropped,
   "She lieth becalmed at sea."

The lovely ladies flocked within,
   And still would each one say,
"Good mercer, be the ships come up?" —
   But still he answered, "Nay."

Then stepped two mariners down the street,
   With looks of grief and fear:
"Now, if Winstanley be your name,
   We bring you evil cheer!

"For the good ship Snowdrop struck, — she struck
   On the rock, — the Eddystone,
And down she went with threescore men,
   We two being left alone.

" Down in the deep with freight and crew,
    Past any help she lies,
And never a bale has come to shore
    Of all thy merchandise."

" For cloth o' gold and comely frieze,"
    Winstanley said and sighed,
" For velvet coif, or costly coat,
    They fathoms deep may bide.

" O thou brave skipper, blithe and kind,
    O mariners, bold and true,
Sorry at heart, right sorry am I,
    A-thinking of yours and you.

" Many long days Winstanley's breast
    Shall feel a weight within,
For a waft of wind he shall be 'feared,
    And trading count but sin.

" To him no more it shall be joy
    To pace the cheerful town,
And see the lovely ladies gay
    Step on in velvet gown."

The Snowdrop sank at Lammas tide,
    All under the yeasty spray ;
On Christmas Eve the brig Content
    Was also cast away.

He little thought o' New Year's night,
　　So jolly as he sat then,
While drank the toast and praised the roast
　　The round-faced Aldermen, —

He little thought on Plymouth Hoe,
　　With every rising tide,
How the wave washed in his sailor lads,
　　And laid them side by side.

There stepped a stranger to the board :
　　" Now, stranger, who be ye ? "
He looked to right, he looked to left,
　　And " Rest you merry," quoth he ;

" For you did not see the brig go down,
　　Or ever a storm had blown ;
For you did not see the white wave rear
　　At the rock, — the Eddystone.

" She drave at the rock with sternsails set ;
　　Crash went the masts in twain ;
She staggered back with her mortal blow,
　　Then leaped at it again.

" There rose a great cry, bitter and strong ;
　　The misty moon looked out !
And the water swarmed with seamen's heads,
　　And the wreck was strewed about.

" I saw her mainsail lash the sea,
  As I clung to the rock alone ;
Then she heeled over, and down she went,
  And sank like any stone.

" She was a fair ship, but all's one !
  For naught could bide the shock." —
" I will take horse," Winstanley said,
  " And see this deadly rock.

" For never again shall bark o' mine
  Sail o'er the windy sea,
Unless, by the blessing of God, for this
  Be found a remedy."

Winstanley rode to Plymouth town
  All in the sleet and the snow ;
And he looked around on shore and sound,
  As he stood on Plymouth Hoe.

Till a pillar of spray rose far away,
  And shot up its stately head,
Reared, and fell over, and reared again :
  " Tis the rock ! the rock ! " he said.

Straight to the Mayor he took his way :
  " Good Master Mayor," quoth he,
" I am a mercer of London town,
  And owner of vessels three.

" But for your rock of dark renown,
   I had five to track the main." —
" You are one of many," the old Mayor said,
   " That of the rock complain.

" An ill rock, mercer! your words ring right,
   Well with my thoughts they chime,
For my two sons to the world to come
   It sent before their time."

" Lend me a lighter, good Master Mayor,
   And a score of shipwrights free;
For I think to raise a lantern tower
   On this rock o' destiny."

The old Mayor laughed, but sighed also:
   " Ah, youth," quoth he, " is rash;
Sooner, young man, thou'lt root it out
   From the sea that doth it lash.

" Who sails too near its jagged teeth,
   He shall have evil lot;
For the calmest seas that tumble there
   Froth like a boiling pot.

" And the heavier seas few look on nigh,
   But straight they lay him dead;
A seventy-gun-ship, sir! — they'll shoot
   Higher than her mast-head.

" Oh, beacons sighted in the dark,
  They are right welcome things,
And pitch-pots flaming on the shore
  Show fair as angel wings.

" Hast gold in hand? then light the land,
  It 'longs to thee and me;
But let alone the deadly rock
  In God Almighty's sea."

Yet said he, " Nay, — I must away,
  On the rock to set my feet;
My debts are paid, my will I made,
  Or ever I did thee greet.

" If I must die, then let me die
  By the rock, and not elsewhere;
If I may live, oh let me live
  To mount my light-house stair."

The old Mayor looked him in the face,
  And answered, " Have thy way:
Thy heart is stout, as if round about
  It was braced with an iron stay:

" Have thy will, mercer! choose thy men,
  Put off from the storm-rid shore;
God with thee be, or I shall see
  Thy face and theirs no more."

Heavily plunged the breaking wave,
   And foam flew up the lea;
Morning and even the drifted snow
   Fell into the dark gray sea.

Winstanley chose him men and gear;
   He said, "My time I waste,"
For the seas ran seething up the shore,
   And the wrack drave on in haste.

But twenty days he waited and more,
   Pacing the strand alone,
Or ever he sat his manly foot
   On the rock, — the Eddystone.

Then he and the sea began their strife,
   And worked with power and might;
Whatever the man reared up by day
   The sea broke down by night.

He wrought at ebb with bar and beam,
   He sailed to shore at flow;
And at his side, by that same tide,
   Came bar and beam also.

" Give in, give in," the old Mayor cried,
   " Or thou wilt rue the day." —
" Yonder he goes," the townsfolk sighed,
   " But the rock will have its way.

" For all his looks that are so stout,
    And his speeches brave and fair,
He may wait on the wind, wait on the wave,
    But he'll build no light-house there."

In fine weather and foul weather
    The rock his arts did flout,
Through the long days and the short days,
    Till all that year ran out.

With fine weather and foul weather
    Another year came in ;
" To take his wage," the workmen said,
    " We almost count a sin."

Now March was gone, came April in,
    And a sea-fog settled down,
And forth sailed he on a glassy sea,
    He sailed from Plymouth town.

With men and stores he put to sea,
  As he was wont to do :
They showed in the fog like ghosts full faint, —
  A ghostly craft and crew.

And the sea-fog lay and waxed alway,
  For a long eight days and more ;
" God help our men," quoth the women then ;
  " For they bide long from shore."

They paced the Hoe in doubt and dread ;
  " Where may our mariners be ? "
But the brooding fog lay soft as down
  Over the quiet sea.

A Scottish schooner made the port,
  The thirteenth day at e'en ;
" As I am a man," the captain cried,
  " A strange sight I have seen :

" And a strange sound heard, my masters all,
  At sea, in the fog and the rain,
Like shipwrights' hammers tapping low,
  Then loud, then low again.

" And a stately house one instant showed,
  Through a rift on the vessel's lea ;
What manner of creatures may be those
  That build upon the sea ? "

Then sighed the folk, " The Lord
    be praised ! "
  And they flocked to the shore
    amain :
All over the Hoe that livelong
    night,
  Many stood out in the rain.

It ceased ; and the red sun reared his head,
　And the rolling fog did flee ;
And, lo ! in the offing faint and far
　Winstanley's house at sea !

In fair weather with mirth and cheer
　The stately tower uprose ;
In foul weather with hunger and cold
　They were content to close ;

Till up the stair Winstanley went,
　To fire the wick afar ;
And Plymouth in the silent night
　Looked out and saw her star.

Winstanley set his foot ashore ;
　Said he, " My work is done ;
I hold it strong to last as long
　As aught beneath the sun.

" But if it fail, as fail it may,
　Borne down with ruin and rout,
Another than I shall rear it high,
　And brace the girders stout.

" A better than I shall rear it high,
　For now the way is plain ;
And though I were dead," Winstanley said,
　" The light would shine again.

" Yet were I fain still to remain,
  Watch in my tower to keep,
And tend my light in the stormiest night
  That ever did move the deep ;

" And if it stood, why then 'twere good,
  Amid their tremulous stirs,
To count each stroke when the mad waves broke,
  For cheers of mariners.

" But if it fell, then this were well,
  That I should with it fall ;
Since, for my part, I have built my heart
  In the courses of its wall.

" Ay ! I were fain, long to remain,
  Watch in my tower to keep,
And tend my light in the stormiest night
  That ever did move the deep."

With that Winstanley went his way,
  And left the rock renowned,
And summer and winter his pilot star
  Hung bright o'er Plymouth Sound.

But it fell out, fell out at last,
  That he would put to sea,
To scan once more his light-house tower
  On the rock o' destiny.

And the winds broke, and the storm broke,
   And wrecks came plunging in ;
None in the town that night lay down
   Or sleep or rest to win.

The great mad waves were rolling graves,
   And each flung up its dead ;
The seething flow was white below,
   And black the sky o'erhead.

And when the dawn, the dull, gray dawn,
   Broke on the trembling town,
And men looked south to the harbor mouth,
   The light-house tower was down.

Down in the deep where he doth sleep,
   Who made it shine afar,
And then in the night that drowned its light,
   Set, with his pilot star.

Many fair tombs in the glorious glooms
   At Westminster they show ;
The brave and the great lie there in state ;
   Winstanley lieth low.

JEAN INGELOW.

THE DEATH OF NELSON.

'Twas in Trafalgar's bay
We saw the Frenchmen lay ;
 Each heart was bounding then.
We scorned the foreign yoke,
Our ships were British oak,
 And hearts of oak our men.
Our Nelson marked them on the wave,
Three cheers our gallant seamen gave,
 Nor thought of home and beauty.
Along the line this signal ran, —
" England expects that every man
 This day will do his duty."

And now the cannons roar
Along the affrighted shore ;
 Brave Nelson led the way :
His ship the Victory named ;
Long be that victory famed !
 For victory crowned the day.

But dearly was that conquest bought,
Too well the gallant hero fought
    For England, home, and beauty.
He cried, as 'midst the fire he ran, —
" England shall find that every man
    This day will do his duty ! "

At last the fatal wound
Which shed dismay around,
    The hero's breast received.
" Heaven fights on our side ;
The day's our own ! " he cried ;
    " Now long enough I've lived.
In honor's cause my life was passed,
In honor's cause I fall at last,
    For England, home, and beauty ! "
Thus ending life as he began ;
England confessed that every man
    That day had done his duty.

ARNOLD.

HOW SLEEP THE BRAVE.

How sleep the brave, who sink to rest
By all their country's wishes blest!
When Spring, with dewy fingers cold,
Returns to deck the hallowed mould,
She there shall dress a sweeter sod
Than Fancy's feet have ever trod.

By fairy hands their knell is rung;
By forms unseen their dirge is sung;
There Honor comes, a pilgrim gray,
To bless the turf that wraps their clay;
And Freedom shall a while repair
To dwell a weeping hermit there!

COLLINS.

CHARADE.

Come from my First, ay, come!
  For the battle-hour is nigh:
And the screaming trump and thundering drum
  Are calling thee to die!

Fight, as tny father fought!
  Fall, as thy father fell!
Thy task is taught, thy shroud is wrought; —
  So — onward — and farewell.

Toll ye my Second, toll!
  Fling wide the flambeau's light,
And sing the hymn for a parted soul
  Beneath the silent night.
With the wreath upon his head,
  And the cross upon his breast,
Let the prayer be said, and the tear be shed: —·
  So — take him to his rest!

Call ye my Whole, — ay, — call
  The lord of lute and lay!
And let him greet the sable pall
  With a noble song to-day.
Ay, call him by his name!
  Nor fitter hand may crave
To light the flame of a soldier's fame
  On the turf of a soldier's grave!

PRAED.

BURIAL OF THE MINNISINK.

ON sunny slope and beechen swell
  The shadowed light of evening fell;
And, where the maple's leaf was brown,
With soft and silent lapse came down
The glory that the wood receives,
At sunset, in its brazen leaves.

Far upward in the mellow light
Rose the blue hills. One cloud of white,
Around a far-uplifted cone,
In the warm blush of evening shone;
An image of the silver lakes
By which the Indian's soul awakes.

But soon a funeral hymn was heard
Where the soft breath of evening stirred
The tall, gray forest; and a band
Of stern in heart, and strong in hand,
Came winding down beside the wave,
To lay the red chief in his grave.

They sang, that by his native bowers
He stood, in the last moon of flowers,
And thirty snows had not yet shed
Their glory on the warrior's head ;
But, as the summer fruit decays,
So died he in those naked days.

A dark cloak of the roebuck's skin
Covered the warrior, and within
Its heavy folds the weapons, made
For the hard toils of war, were laid ;
The cuirass, woven of plaited reeds,
And the broad belt of shells and beads.

Before, a dark-haired virgin train
Chanted the death-dirge of the slain ;
Behind, the long procession came
Of hoary men and chiefs of fame,
With heavy hearts, and eyes of grief,
Leading the war-horse of their chief.

Stripped of his proud and martial dress,
Uncurbed, unreined, and riderless,
With darting eye and nostril spread,
And heavy and impatient tread,
He came ; and oft that eye so proud
Asked for his rider in the crowd.

They buried the dark chief; they freed
Beside the grave his battle-steed;
And swift an arrow cleaved its way
To his stern heart! One piercing neigh
Arose, — and, on the dead man's plain,
The rider grasps his steed again.

LONGFELLOW.

———∞○◦○∞———

MY KATE.

———

I.

She was not as pretty as women I know,
And yet all your best made of sunshine and snow
Drop to shade, melt to nought in the long-trodden ways,
While she's still remembered on warm and cold days —
My Kate.

II.

Her air had a meaning, her movements a grace;
You turned from the fairest to gaze on her face:
And when you had once seen her forehead and mouth,
You saw as distinctly her soul and her truth —
My Kate.

III.

Such a blue inner light from her eyelids outbroke,
You looked at her silence and fancied she spoke :
When she did, so peculiar yet soft was the tone,
Though the loudest spoke also, you heard her alone —
                              My Kate.

IV.

I doubt if she said to you much that could act
As a thought or suggestion ; she did not attract
In the sense of the brilliant or wise ; I infer
'Twas her thinking of others made you think of her —
                              My Kate.

V.

She never found fault with you, never implied
Your wrong by her right ; and yet men at her side
Grew nobler, girls purer, as through the whole town
The children were gladder that pulled at her gown —
                              My Kate.

VI.

None knelt at her feet confessed lovers in thrall ;
They knelt more to God than they used, — that was all :
If you praised her as charming, some asked what you
      meant,
But the charm of her presence was felt when she went —
                              My Kate.

VII.

The weak and the gentle, the ribald and rude,
She took as she found them, and did them all good ;
It always was so with her — see what you have !
She has made the grass greener even here . . . with her
    grave —

                 My Kate.

VIII.

My dear one ! — when thou wast alive with the rest,
I held thee the sweetest and loved thee the best :
And now thou art dead, shall I not take thy part
As thy smiles used to do for thyself, my sweet Heart —

                 My Kate.

                    Mrs. Browning.

DAYBREAK.

A wind came up out of the sea,
And said, " O mists, make room for me."

It hailed the ships, and cried, " Sail on,
Ye mariners, the night is gone."

And hurried landward far away,
Crying, " Awake ! it is the day."

It said unto the forest, " Shout !
Hang all your leafy banners out ! "

It touched the wood-bird's folded wing,
And said, " O bird, awake and sing ! "

And o'er the farms, " O chanticleer !
Your clarion blow ; the day is near."

It whispered to the fields of corn,
" Bow down, and hail the coming morn."

It shouted through the belfry-tower,
" Awake, O bell ! proclaim the hour."

It crossed the church-yard with a sigh,
And said, " Not yet ! in quiet lie."

LONGFELLOW.

FLOWERS.

WE are the sweet flowers,
        Born of sunny showers,
      (Think, whene'er you see us, what our beauty
            saith ;)
        Utterance mute and bright,
        Of some unknown delight,
We fill the air with pleasure by our simple breath ;
        All who see us love us, —
        We befit all places ;
Unto sorrow we give smiles, and unto graces, graces.

        Mark our ways, how noiseless
        All, and sweetly voiceless,
Though the March-winds pipe, to make our passage
            clear ;
        Not a whisper tells
        Where our small seed dwells,
Nor is known the moment green when our tips appear.
        We thread the earth in silence,
        In silence build our bowers, —
And leaf by leaf in silence show, till we laugh a-top,
            sweet flowers.

                                        LEIGH HUNT.

THE USE OF FLOWERS.

God might have bade the earth bring forth
   Enough for great and small,
The oak-tree and the cedar-tree,
   Without a flower at all.

We might have had enough, enough
   For every want of ours,
For luxury, medicine, and toil,
   And yet have had no flowers.

The ore within the mountain mine
   Requireth none to grow ;
Nor doth it need the lotus-flower
   To make the river flow.

The clouds might give abundant rain,
   The nightly dews might fall,
And the herb that keepeth life in man
   Might yet have drunk them all.

Then wherefore, wherefore were they made,
   All dyed with rainbow light,
All fashioned with supremest grace,
   Upspringing day and night, —

Springing in valleys green and low,
   And on the mountain high,
And in the silent wilderness,
   Where no man passes by?

Our outward life requires them not,
   Then wherefore had they birth? —
To minister delight to man,
   To beautify the earth;

To comfort man, to whisper hope
   Whene'er his faith is dim;
For Whoso careth for the flowers
   Will much more care for him.

MARY HOWITT.

THE PALM–TREE.

Is it the palm, the cocoa-palm,
On the Indian sea by the isles of balm?
Or is it a ship in the breezeless calm?

A ship whose keel is of palm beneath,
Whose ribs of palm have a palm-bark sheath,
And a rudder of palm it steereth with.

Branches of palm are its spars and rails.
Fibres of palm are its woven sails,
And the rope is of palm that idly trails.

What does the good ship bear so well?
The cocoa-nut with its stony shell,
And the milky sap of its inner cell.

What are its jars, so smooth and fine,
But hollowed nuts, filled with oil and wine,
And the cabbage that ripens under the Line?

The master he sits on a palm-mat soft,
From a beaker of palm his drink is quaffed,
And a palm-thatch shields from the sun aloft.

His dress is woven of palmy strands,
And he holds a palm-leaf scroll in his hands,
Traced with the Prophet's wise commands.

The turban folded about his head
Was daintily wrought of the palm-leaf braid,
And the fan that cools him of palm was made.

Of threads of palm was the carpet spun
Whereon he kneels when the day is done,
And the foreheads of Islam are bowed as one!

To him the palm is a gift divine,
Wherein all uses of man combine, —
House, and raiment, and food, and wine.

And, in the hour of his great release,
His need of the palm shall only cease
With the shroud wherein he lieth in peace.

" Allah il Allah ! " he sings his psalm,
On the Indian sea, by the isles of balm ;
" Thanks to Allah who gives the palm ! "

WHITTIER.

THE   EMPEROR'S   BIRD'S-NEST.

ONCE the Emperor Charles of Spain
　　With his swarthy, grave commanders,
I forget in what campaign,
Long besieged in mud and rain
　　Some old frontier town in Flanders.

Up and down the dreary camp,
　　In great boots of Spanish leather,
Striding with a measured tramp,
These Hidalgos, dull and damp,
　　Cursed the Frenchmen, cursed the weather.

Thus as to and fro they went,
　　Over upland and through hollow,
Giving their impatience vent,
Perched upon the Emperor's tent,
　　In her nest, they spied a swallow.

Yes, it was a swallow's nest,
　　Built of clay and hair of horses,
Mane or tail, or dragoon's crest,
Found on hedge-rows east and west,
　　After skirmish of the forces.

" Let no hand the bird molest,"
    Said the Emperor, " nor hurt her ! "
Adding then, by way of jest,
" Golondrina [1] is my guest,
    'Tis the wife of some deserter ! "

Swift as bow-string speeds a shaft,
    Through the camp was spread the rumor,
And the soldiers, as they quaffed
Flemish beer at dinner, laughed
    At the Emperor's pleasant humor.

So unarmed and unafraid
    Sat the swallow still and brooded,
Till the constant cannonade
Through the walls a breach had made,
    And the siege was thus concluded.

Then the army, elsewhere bent,
    Struck its tents as if disbanding,
Only not the Emperor's tent,
For he ordered, ere he went,
    Very curtly, " Leave it standing ! "

---

[1] Swallow.   Also meaning a deserter.

So it stood there all alone,
  Loosely flapping, torn, and tattered,
Till the brood was fledged and flown,
Singing o'er those walls of stone
  Which the cannon-shot had shattered.

LONGFELLOW.

TO A REDBREAST.

Little bird, with bosom red,
Welcome to my humble shed!
Courtly domes of high degree
Have no room for thee or me;
Pride and pleasure's fickle throng
Nothing mind an idle song.
Daily near my table steal,
While I pick my scanty meal.
Doubt not, little though there be,
But I'll cast a crumb to thee,
Well rewarded if I spy
Pleasure in thy glancing eye;
See thee, when thou'st eat thy fill,
Plume thy breast, and wipe thy bill.
Come, my feathered friend, again,
Well thou know'st the broken pane.

LANGHORNE.

THE BEGGAR.

A beggar through this world am I,
From place to place I wander by;
Fill up my pilgrim's scrip for me,
For Christ's sweet sake and charity!
    A little of thy steadfastness,
Rounded with leafy gracefulness,
Old oak, give me, —
That the world's blasts may round me blow,
And I yield gently to and fro,
While my stout-hearted trunk below,
And firm-set roots, unmovéd be.
    Some of thy stern, unyielding might,
Enduring still through day and night
Rude tempest-shock and withering blight, —
That I may keep at bay
The changeful April sky of chance,
And the strong tide of circumstance, —
Give me, old granite gray.
    Some of thy mournfulness serene,
Some of the never-dying green,

Put in this scrip of mine, —
That grief may fall like snow-flakes light,
And deck me in a robe of white,
Ready to be an angel bright, —
O sweetly mournful pine !

  A little of thy merriment,
Of thy sparkling, light content,
Give me, my cheerful brook, —
That I may still be full of glee
And gladsomeness, where'er I be,
Though fickle fate hath prisoned me
In some neglected nook.

  Ye have been very kind and good
To me, since I have been in the wood ;
Ye have gone nigh to fill my heart ;
But good-by, kind friends, every one,
I've far to go ere set of sun :
Of all good things I would have part,
The day was high ere I could start,
And so my journey's scarce begun.

  Heaven help me ! how could I forget
To beg of thee, dear violet ?
Some of thy modesty,
That flowers here as well, unseen,
As if before the world thou'dst been,
  Oh, give, to strengthen me.

J. R. LOWELL.

JOHN BARLEYCORN.

There went three kings into the East,
  Three kings both great and high ;
And they have sworn a solemn oath,
  John Barleycorn shall die.

They took a plough and ploughed him down,
  Put clods upon his head ;
And they have sworn a solemn oath,
  John Barleycorn was dead.

But the cheerful spring came kindly on,
  And showers began to fall ;
John Barleycorn got up again,
  And sore surprised them all.

The sultry suns of summer came,
  And he grew thick and strong ;
His head well armed with pointed spears,
  That no one should him wrong.

The sober autumn entered mild,
  And he grew wan and pale ;
His bending joints and drooping head
  Showed he began to fail.

His color sickened more and more,
   He faded into age ;
And then his enemies began
   To show their deadly rage.

They took a weapon long and sharp,
   And cut him by the knee ;
Then tied him fast upon a cart,
   Like a rogue for forgery.

They laid him down upon his back,
   And cudgelled him full sore ;
They hung him up before the storm,
   And turned him o'er and o'er.

They filled up then a darksome pit
   With water to the brim.
And heaved in poor John Barleycorn,
   To let him sink or swim.

They laid him out upon the floor,
   To work him further woe ;
And still as signs of life appeared,
   They tossed him to and fro.

They wasted o'er a scorching flame
   The marrow of his bones ;
But the miller used him worst of all,
   For he crushed him between two stones.

And they have taken his very heart's blood,
   And drunk it round and round ;
And so farewell, John Barleycorn !
   Thy fate thou now hast found.

BURNS.

————o○º◦º○o————

THERE WAS A JOLLY MILLER.

————

There was a jolly miller once lived on the river Dee,
He danced and sung from morn till night, — no lark so
    blithe as he ;
And this the burden of his song forever used to be :
" I care for nobody, no, not I, if nobody cares for me.

" I live by my mill, God bless her ! she's kindred, child,
    and wife ;
I would not change my station for any other in life ;
No lawyer, surgeon, or doctor, e'er had a groat from me ;
I care for nobody, no, not I, if nobody cares for me."

When spring begins his merry career, oh, how his heart
    grows gay !
No summer's drought alarms his fears, nor winter's cold
    decay ;

No foresight mars the miller's joy, who's wont to sing
    and say:
" Let others toil from year to year, I live from day to
    day."

Thus, like the miller, bold and free, let us rejoice and
    sing,
The days of youth are made for glee, and time is on the
    wing,
This song shall pass from me to thee, along the jovial
    ring, —
Let heart and voice, and all agree, to say, " Long live
    the king ! "

BICKERSTAFFE.

THE FRIAR OF ORDERS GRAY.

It was a friar of orders gray
    Walked forth to tell his beads;
And he met with a lady fair,
    Clad in a pilgrim's weeds.

" Now Christ thee save, thou reverend friar !
    I pray thee tell to me,
If ever at yon holy shrine
    My true-love thou didst see."

" And how should I know your true-love
    From many another one ? " —
" Oh, by his cockle-hat and staff,
    And by his sandal shoon.

" But chiefly by his face and mien,
    That were so fair to view ;
His flaxen locks that sweetly curled,
    And eyes of lovely blue."

" O lady, he is dead and gone !
    Lady, he's dead and gone !
And at his head a green grass turf,
    And at his heels a stone.

" Within these holy cloisters long
  He languished, and he died
Lamenting of a lady's love,
  And 'plaining of her pride.

" They bore him barefaced on his bier,
  Six proper youths and tall,
And many a tear bedewed his grave
  Within yon kirk-yard wall."

" And art thou dead, thou gentle youth;
  And art thou dead and gone?
And didst thou die for love of me?
  Break, cruel heart of stone ! "

" Oh, weep not, lady, weep not so,
  Some ghostly comfort seek ;
Let not vain sorrow rive thy heart,
  Nor tears bedew thy cheek."

" Oh, do not, do not, holy friar,
  My sorrow now reprove ;
For I have lost the sweetest youth
  That e'er won lady's love.

" And now, alas ! for thy sad loss
  I'll ever weep and sigh ;
For thee I only wished to live,
  For thee I wish to die."

" Weep no more, lady, weep no more,
  Thy sorrow is in vain ;
For violets plucked the sweetest showers
  Will ne'er make grow again."

" Oh, say not so, thou holy friar,
  I pray thee say not so ;
For since my true-love died for me,
  'Tis meet my tears should flow.

" And will he never come again ?
  Will he ne'er come again ?
Ah, no ! he is dead and laid in his grave,
  Forever to remain.

" His cheek was redder than the rose ;
  The comeliest youth was he ;
But he is dead and laid in his grave :
  Alas, and woe is me ! "

" Sigh no more, lady, sigh no more ;
  Men were deceivers ever ;
One foot on sea and one on shore,
  To one thing constant never.

" Hadst thou been fond, he had been false,
  And left thee sad and heavy ;
For young men ever were fickle found,
  Since summer-trees were leafy."

" Now say not so, thou holy friar,
  I pray thee say not so ;
My love he had the truest heart,
  Oh, he was ever true !

" And art thou dead, thou much-loved youth,
  And didst thou die for me ?
Then, farewell home ; for evermore
  A pilgrim I will be.

' But first upon my true-love's grave
  My weary limbs I'll lay,
And thrice I'll kiss the green grass turf
  That wraps his breathless clay."

" Yet stay, fair lady, rest awhile   ·
  Beneath this cloister wall ;
See, through the hawthorn blows the wind,
  And drizzly rain doth fall."

" Oh, stay me not, thou holy friar,
  Oh, stay me not, I pray !
No drizzly rain that falls on me
  Can wash my fault away."

" Yet stay, fair lady, turn again,
  And dry those pearly tears ;
For see, beneath this gown of gray
  Thy own true-love appears.

' Here, forced by grief and hopeless love,
   These holy weeds I sought,
And here amid these lonely walls
   To end my days I thought.

" But haply, for my year of grace
   Is not yet passed away,
Might I still hope to win thy love,
   No longer would I stay."

" Now farewell grief, and welcome joy,
   Once more unto my heart;
For since I've found thee, lovely youth,
   We never more will part."

                           PERCY.

BLOW, BLOW, THOU WINTER WIND.

————

Blow, blow, thou winter wind!
Thou art not so unkind
　　As man's ingratitude!
Thy tooth is not so keen,
Because thou art not seen,
　　Although thy breath be rude.
Heigh, ho! sing heigh, ho! unto the green holly,
Most friendship is feigning, most loving mere folly.
　　Then heigh, ho! the holly!
　　This life is most jolly!

Freeze, freeze, thou bitter sky!
Thou dost not bite so nigh
　　As benefits forgot!
Though thou the waters warp,
Thy sting is not so sharp
　　As friend remembered not.
Heigh, ho! etc., etc.

SHAKESPEARE.

LLEWELLYN AND HIS DOG.

The spearmen heard the bugle sound,
   And cheer'ly smiled the morn;
And many a dog, and many a hound,
   Attend Llewellyn's horn.

And still he blew a louder blast,
   And gave a louder cheer;
" Come, Gelert! why art thou the last
   Llewellyn's horn to hear?

" Oh, where does faithful Gelert roam,
   The flower of all his race?
So true, so brave — a lamb at home,
   A lion in the chase."

That day Llewellyn little loved
   The chase of hart or hare,
And scant and small the booty proved,
   For Gelert was not there.

Unpleased, Llewellyn homeward hied,
   When, near the portal seat,
His truant Gelert he espied,
   Bounding his lord to greet.

But when he gained the castle door,
   Aghast the chieftain stood;
The hound was smeared with gouts of gore,
   His lips and fangs ran blood!

Llewellyn gazed with wild surprise;
   Unused such looks to meet,
His fav'rite checked his joyful guise,
   And crouched, and licked his feet.

Onward in haste Llewellyn passed
   (And on went Gelert too),
And still, where'er his eyes were cast,
   Fresh blood-gouts shocked his view!

O'erturned his infant's bed he found,
   The blood-stained cover rent;
And all around the walls and ground
   With recent blood besprent.

He called his child — no voice replied;
   He searched with terror wild;
Blood! blood! he found on every side,
   But nowhere found his child!

" Hell-hound! by thee my child's devoured! "
   The frantic father cried;
And to the hilt his vengeful sword
   He plunged in Gelert's side.

His suppliant, as to earth he fell,
  No pity could impart;
But still his Gelert's dying yell
  Passed heavy o'er his heart.

Aroused by Gelert's dying yell,
  Some slumberer wakened nigh;
What words the parent's joy can tell,
  To hear his infant cry!

Concealed beneath a mangled heap,
　His hurried search had missed,
All glowing from his rosy sleep,
　His cherub boy he kissed!

Nor scratch had he, nor harm, nor dread,
　But the same couch beneath
Lay a great wolf, all torn and dead, —
　Tremendous still in death!

Ah, what was then Llewellyn's pain!
　For now the truth was clear;
The gallant hound the wolf had slain,
　To save Llewellyn's heir.

Vain, vain was all Llewellyn's woe;
　" Best of thy kind, adieu!
The frantic deed which laid thee low
　This heart shall ever rue!"

And now a gallant tomb they raised,
　With costly sculpture decked;
And marbles storied with his praise
　Poor Gelert's bones protect.

Here never could the spearman pass,
　Or forester, unmoved,
Here oft the tear-besprinkled grass
　Llewellyn's sorrow proved.

And here he hung his horn and spear,
   And oft, as evening fell,
In fancy's piercing sounds would hear
   Poor Gelert's dying yell.

SOUTHEY.

—○○⦂○⦂○○—

THE BOAT OF GRASS.

For years the slave endured his yoke,
   Down-trodden, wronged, misused, oppressed ;
Yet life-long serfdom could not choke
   The seeds of freedom in his breast.

At length, upon the north wind came
   A whisper stealing through the land ;
It spread from hut to hut like flame, —
   " Take heart : the hour is near at hand ! "

The whisper spread, and lo ! on high
   The dawn of an unhoped-for day !
" Be glad : the Northern troops are nigh, —
   The fleet is in Port-Royal Bay ! "

Responsive to the words of cheer,
   An inner voice said, " Rise and flee !
Be strong, and cast away all fear :
   Thou art a man, and thou art free ! "

And, full of new-born hope and might,
　He started up, and seaward fled :
By day he turned aside ; by night
　He followed where the North Star led.

Through miles of barren pine and waste,
　And endless breadth of swamp and sedge,
By streams, whose winding path is traced
　In tangled growth along their edge ;

Two nights he fled, — no sound was heard,
　He met no creature on his way ;
Two days crouched in the bush ; the third,
　He hears the blood-hounds' distant bay.

They drag him back to stripes and shame,
　And bitter, unrequited toil ;
With red-hot chains his feet they maim,
　All future thought of flight to foil.

But the celestial voice, that spake
　Clear in his soul, might not be hushed ;
The sense of birthright, once awake,
　Could never, never more be crushed.

And, brave of heart and strong of will,
　He kept his purpose, laid his plan ;
Though crippled, chained, and captive still,
　A slave no longer, but a man.

Eleven months his soul he steeled
    To toil and wait in silent pain,
But in the twelfth his wounds were healed, —
    He burst his bonds, and fled again.

A weary winding stream he sought,
    And crossed its waters to and fro, —
An Indian wile, to set at nought
    The bloody instinct of his foe.

The waters widen to a fen,
  And, — while he hid him, breathless, there, —
With brutal cries of dogs and men,
  The hunt went round and round his lair.

The baffled hounds had lost the track :
  With many a curse and many a cry
The angry owners called them back ;
  And so the wild pursuit went by.

The deadly peril seemed to pass ;
  And then he dared to raise his head
Above the waving swampy grass,
  That mantled o'er the river-bed.

Those long broad leaves that round him grew
  He had been wont to bind and plait ;
And well, with simple skill, he knew
  To shape the basket and the mat.

Now, in their tresses sad and dull
  He saw the hope of his escape,
And patiently began to cull,
  And weave them in canoe-like shape.

To give the reedy fabric slight
  An armor 'gainst the soaking brine,
With painful care he sought by night
  The amber weepings of the pine.

And, since on the Egyptian wave
  The Hebrew launched her little ark,
Faith never to God's keeping gave
  So great a hope, so frail a bark.

O silent river of the South,
  Whose lonely stream ne'er felt the oar
In all its course, from rise to mouth,
  What precious freight was that you bore !

But still the boat, from dawn to dark,
  'Neath overhanging shrubs was drawn :
And, loosed at eve, the little bark
  Safe floated on from dark to dawn.

At length, in that mysterious hour
  That comes before the break of day,
The current gained a swifter power,
  The boat began to rock and sway.

He felt the wave beneath him swell,
  His nostrils drank a fresh salt breath,
The boat of rushes rose and fell ; —
  " Lord ! is it life, or is it death ? "

He saw the eastern heaven spanned
  With a slow-spreading belt of gray ;
Tents glimmered, ghost-like, on the sand ;
  And phantom ships before him lay.

The sky grew bright, the day awoke,
　　The sun flashed up above the sea,
From countless drum and bugle broke
　　The joyous Northern reveillé.

O white-winged warriors of the deep!
　　No heart e'er hailed you so before:
No castaway on desert steep,
　　Nor banished man, his exile o'er,

Nor drowning wretch lashed to a spar,
　　So blessed your rescuing sails as he
Who on them first beheld from far
　　The morning-light of Liberty!

MRS. WISTER.

HE PRAYETH WELL WHO LOVETH WELL.

Oh, sweeter than the marriage-feast,
  'Tis sweeter far to me
To walk together to the kirk,
  With a goodly company !

To walk together to the kirk,
  And all together pray,
While each to his great Father bends, —
Old men, and babes, and loving friends,
  And youths and maidens gay.

Farewell, farewell ! but this I tell
  To thee, thou wedding-guest !
He prayeth well who loveth well
  Both man, and bird, and beast.

He prayeth best who loveth best
  All things both great and small ;
For the dear God who loveth us,
  He made and loveth all.

COLERIDGE.

GOOD-NIGHT, GOOD-BY.

Say not good-by!   Dear friend, from thee
A word too sad that word would be.
Say not good-by!   Say but good-night,
And say it with thy tender, light,
Caressing voice, that links the bliss
Of yet another day with this.
     Say but good-night!

Say not good-by!   Say but good-night:
A word that blesses in its flight,
In leaving hope of many a kind,
Sweet day, like this we leave behind.
Say but good-night!   Oh, never say
A word that taketh thee away!
     Say but good-night!   Good-night!

DORA GREENWELL.

LIFE.

Life ! I know not what thou art,
But know that thou and I must part;
And when, or how, or where we met,
I own to me's a secret yet.

Life, we have been long together,
Through pleasant and through cloudy weather;
'Tis hard to part where friends are dear,
Perhaps 'twill cost a sigh, a tear.
Then steal away, give little warning;
        Choose thine own time;
Say not Good-night, but in some brighter clime
        Bid me Good-morning.

MRS. BARBAULD.

THE BETTER LAND.

" I hear thee speak of the better land;
Thou call'st its children a happy band;
Mother! oh, where is that radiant shore?
Shall we not seek it, and weep no more?

Is it where the flower of the orange blows,
And the fire-flies dance through the myrtle
      boughs?" —
  " Not there, not there, my child!"

" Is it where the feathery palm-trees rise,
And the date grows ripe under sunny skies?
Or midst the green islands of glittering seas,
Where fragrant forests perfume the breeze,

And strange bright birds on their starry wings
Bear the rich hues of all glorious things?" —
    " Not there, not there, my child!"

" Is it far away, in some region old,
Where the rivers wander o'er sands of gold?
Where the burning rays of the ruby shine,
And the diamond lights up the secret mine,
And the pearl gleams forth from the coral strand?
Is it there, sweet mother, that better land?" —
    " Not there, not there, my child!

" Eye hath not seen it, my gentle boy;
Ear hath not heard its deep songs of joy;
Dreams cannot picture a world so fair, —
Sorrow and death may not enter there;
Time doth not breathe on its fadeless bloom;
For beyond the clouds and beyond the tomb,
    It is there, it is there, my child!"

MRS. HEMANS.

HEAVEN.

———

Oh, what is this splendor that beams on me now,
   This beautiful sunrise that dawns on my soul,
While faint and far off land and sea lie below,
    And under my feet the huge golden clouds roll?

To what mighty king doth this city belong,
    With its rich jewelled shrines, and its gardens of
       flowers;
With its breaths of sweet incense, its measures of song,
    And the light that is gilding its numberless towers?

And, oh, if the exiles of earth could but win
    One sight of the beauty of Jesus above,
From that hour they would cease to be able to sin,
    And earth would be heaven; for heaven is love.

                                  FABER.

THE CHILD'S DESIRE.

I think, as I read that sweet story of old,
   When Jesus was here among men,
How He called little children as lambs to His fold,
   I should like to have been with them then.
I wish that His hands had been placed on my head,
   That His arms had been thrown around me,
And that I might have seen His kind look when He said,
   " Let the little ones come unto me."

But still to His footstool in prayer I may go,
   And ask for a share in His love;
And if I thus earnestly seek Him below,
   I shall see Him and hear Him above,
In that beautiful place He has gone to prepare
   For all that are washed and forgiven;
And many dear children are gathering there,
   " For of such is the kingdom of heaven."

                                 MRS. LUKE.

CHILDREN, THANK GOD.

Children, thank God for these great trees,
That fan the land with every breeze;
Whose drooping branches form cool bowers
Where you can spend the summer hours, —
For these thank God.

For fragrant sweets of blossoms bright,
Whose beauty gives you such delight;
For the soft grass beneath your feet,
For new-mown hay, and clover sweet, —
For all thank God.

The very cows, that lie and doze
Beneath the trees in glad repose ;
The birds, that in their branches sing,
And make the air with music ring,
    All these thank God.

Oh, thank God for the radiant sky,
Whose varying beauty charms the eye, —
Now gray and dark, now blue and bright,
Unfailing source of pure delight, —
    For this thank God.

He gives the life to everything, —
To beasts that roar, and birds that sing.
But thought and speech he gave to men,
While beasts are dumb : O children, then,
    For this thank God !

RHYMING STORY-BOOK.

DATE			